ULTIMATE YOUTH SHOOTiNG SPORTS gUiDE

BY DAVE AND STEVE SHELLHAAS

MIAMI VALLEY OUTDOOR MEDIA, LTD.

The *Ultimate Youth Shooting Sports Guide* was supported by conservation organizations that believe in introducing the next generation to the shooting sports and other outdoor traditions.

Pheasants Forever and Quail Forever

 Pheasants Forever (founded 1982) and *Quail Forever* (founded 2005) work with their members, chapters and partners to provide opportunities for youth and their families to enjoy the outdoors and develop a conservation ethic. Their No Child Left Indoors® initiative supports local programs that include shooting sports, mentor hunts, family outdoor days, youth pollinator projects, camp experiences and youth leadership training. They sponsor the National Youth Leadership Council comprised of youth from around the country who serve as spokespersons for their age group on conservation issues. PF/QF chapters host more than a thousand events every year that involve 100,000 youth and adults. The Forever Shooting Sports program has raised over $4 million for shooting team endowments.

Youth who become a Ringnecks (PF) youth member or a Whistlers (QF) youth member for $15 per year will receive a quarterly magazine *Forever Outdoors* and an introduction to their local chapter.

For more information, go to: www.PheasantsForever.org or www.QuailForever.org.

Hunter Legacy 100 Fund (HLF) -
Safari Club International (SCI) &
Safari Club International Foundation

 *Safari Club International* is a national membership organization with a conservation focus. It is First for Hunters. Its mission is to be a strong advocate on behalf of all hunters to maintain our freedom to hunt and to support sustainable science based conservation. SCI Chapters around the world are involved in educating youth in their communities in hunter education and shooting sports.

HLF is a group of Safari Club International members who formed and funded the HLF as a way to provide financial support for conservation and education programs that contribute to the continuation of our hunting heritage. It provided funds in partnership with Pheasants Forever to develop, to publish and to distribute this Ultimate Youth Shooting Sports Guide.

HLF operates within Safari Club International Foundation. SCI Foundation is a 501(3) nonprofit that is First for Wildlife through support of science based conservation research and projects and through education of next generations. SCI Foundation partners with 4-H National Shooting Sports, The Salvation Army Outdoors, National Archery in the Schools Program and Boy Scouts of America Venturing in bringing conservation education lessons, shooting sports and hunting to tens of thousands of youth each year.

SCI Foundation owns and operates the American Wilderness Leadership School (AWLS) near Jackson, WY. AWLS summer high school program offers young hunters and shooting sports enthusiasts' opportunity to learn about the North American Model of Wildlife Conservation and to learn leadership and advocacy skills. AWLS provides professional development courses in conservation, shooting sports and hunting for school teachers.

CONTENTS

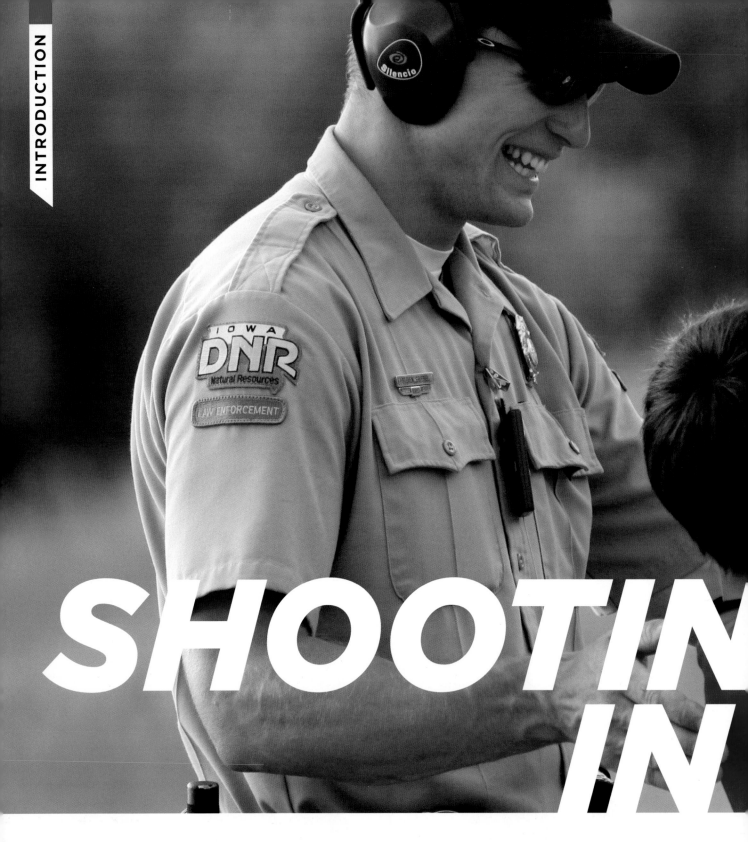

SHOOTIN IN

Sports are a big part of our society. Turn on the television and you will see all types of sporting events. There are many sports that young people can choose. However, many sports favor participants that are strong, fast, or a certain size. Although many youth dream about being in the NBA, NFL, WNBA, or on a World Cup soccer team, very few have the size and natural talent to reach those levels.

G SPORTS AMERICA

There are sports

where you can become very successful no matter how big or strong you are, or whether you are a guy or a girl. You can also be good at these sports no matter when you start. Another great thing about these sports is that you can continue to enjoy them long into your adult life. So, what sports are they? **The Shooting Sports!!**

Shooting sports are actually some of the fastest growing activities in the United States for many of the same reasons that were just stated, and more. The shooting sports can be enjoyed by the whole family and are one of the safest sports.

Shooting Sports Are Not New

Shooting sports in America date back to the 1700s. Shooting was an important part of surviving as people set out into the new frontier. Shooting accurately was important for protection and to hunt for food.

As settlers practiced their shooting skills, the first competitions were "turkey shoots" where shooters would shoot one shot and the shooter closest to the "mark" would win food, usually a turkey, or sometimes other meat or food.

In the 1800s, there were organized shooting matches where people would travel to events and compete. These matches were very popular and crowds would come to watch the competition. A match in Glendale Park, NY, in the 1880s brought 600 shooters and 30,000 spectators. Now that was a big sporting event for that time period!

Photo credit: Courtesy of Garst Museum and The National Annie Oakley Center, Greenville, OH

Little Sure Shot

One of the best known shooters in American history was a girl named Annie Oakley. Annie Oakley actually was her stage name. She was born Phoebe Ann Moses in Darke County, Ohio, in 1860. She sharpened her shooting skills by hunting game for a grocery store. She was such a good shot, she earned enough money to pay off the mortgage on her mother's home by the time she was 15.

She eventually went on to marry another top shooter in America, Frank Butler. In 1884, Annie met the Native-American Chief Sitting Bull and he was so impressed by her shooting skills he gave her the name "Little Sure Shot." Together they joined Buffalo Bill's Wild West Show in 1885. She traveled the nation wowing audiences with her unbelievable marksmanship.

Check out these awesome shots:

- She could shoot the thin edge of a playing card from 30 yards.
- She could shoot far away targets while facing the opposite direction using a mirror.
- She could shoot holes in playing cards that were thrown up in the air.

Now those tricks give a new meaning to "you shoot like a girl!" Most men at the time, and even today, cannot match these incredible shots. That is the great thing about shooting sports, anyone can be a great shot with the right technique and practice.

Photo credit: Courtesy of Garst Museum and The National Annie Oakley Center, Greenville, OH

"You shoot like a girl!"
–Thank you!

What are Shooting

Definition:

competitive sports that use firearms or airguns

Shooting Sports Facts:

➤ Over 19 million Americans participate in target shooting!

➤ 20-40 million Americans are recreational shooters.

There are many types of shooting sports for young people to get involved. You can explore the shooting sports with inexpensive equipment or get involved in a shooting club that will provide you with the equipment you need.

By participating in shooting sports, you learn and develop the following skills and qualities:

- Gun safety and respect
- Increased concentration and mental toughness
- Discipline to practice and compete
- Enjoyment of an activity you can participate in for the rest of your life

Sports?

Shooting sports can be enjoyed as an individual or team sport. You can participate on your own in individual competitions or on a team. You can also enjoy shooting sports as a fun, family activity. The great thing about shooting sports is that you can enjoy the sports for a lifetime. Many other sports are sometimes difficult to participate in as people get older, but not shooting sports.

➤ *Air gun shooting*
➤ *Rifle and Pistol shooting*
➤ *Muzzleloader and Cowboy Action shooting*
➤ *Trap, Skeet, and Sporting Clays*
➤ *Archery*

Did you know hunting is actually considered a shooting sport? Hunting involves the same aspects of other shooting sports, except the target involves a game animal.

A game animal is any animal that is harvested and managed by state and federal regulations and seasons.

How safe are shooting sports???

Shooting sports are as safe or safer than most other traditional sports. Here is a result of a study of sports injuries in the U.S.:

SPORTS INJURY STUDY
Total Injuries Ranked by Sport

Numbers are in thousands (000)

Sport Total	Total Sport Participants	Injured Participants	% of Total Injuries	Injuries Per 100 Participants
TOTAL INJURIES	**211,202**	**20,145**	**100.0**	**9.5**
Basketball	36,584	2,783	13.8	7.6
Running/Jogging	35,866	1,654	8.2	4.6
Soccer	17,641	1,634	8.1	9.3
Football (tackle)	5,783	1,084	5.4	18.8
Baseball	10,402	602	3.0	5.8
Bicycling (recreational)	53,524	445	2.2	0.8
Tennis	16,353	415	2.1	2.5
Ice Hockey	2,612	415	2.1	15.9
Skateboarding	12,997	399	2.0	3.1
Walking (recreational)	84,986	384	1.9	0.5
Golf	27,812	291	1.4	1.0
Hunting	**16,471**	**207**	**1.0**	**1.3**
Gymnastics	5,149	149	0.7	2.9
Ice Skating	14,530	105	0.5	0.7
Swimming (recreational)	92,667	73	0.4	0.1
Bowling	53,160	50	0.2	0.1
Paintball	**8,679**	**21**	**0.1**	**0.2**
Shooting (trap & skeet)	**3,696**	**16**	**0.1**	**0.4**
Archery	**6,650**	**16**	**0.1**	**0.2**
Canoeing	10,933	11	0.1	0.1

Source: American Sports Data, Inc. - A Comprehensive Study of Sports Injuries in the U.S.

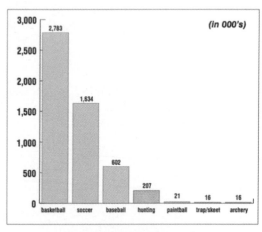

Comparison of Number of Participants Injured

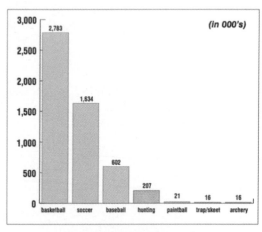

2006 Industry Reference Guide

A Brief History of Conservation in America
"The importance of Shooting, Hunting, and Angling to Conservation"

Conservation:

The wise and intelligent use and management of natural resources.

Do you enjoy the forests and all of the wildlife that call these wild places home? We all do!! America has wonderful natural resources such as forests and abundant wildlife. However, it has not always been that way.

Back in the early days of our nation, people were settling this new land and really changing the landscape. People also hunted the wildlife for food and to sell for money. This eventually caused many game animals to become very scarce. In the early 1900s, President Teddy Roosevelt realized that our nation had to manage and conserve our natural resources. As a hunter, angler, and a great outdoorsman, President Roosevelt understood that these resources had to be conserved so everyone could enjoy them long into the future.

President Roosevelt began this conservation effort by creating the National Forest Service to manage and protect our great forests. He also began the practice of scientifically managing wildlife and other natural resources. These practices are still used today.

What is the North American Model of Wildlife Conservation?

When conservation-minded people became concerned about disappearing wildlife, they began working to preserve wildlife and their habitats. Their efforts were the source of the North American Model, which strives to sustain wildlife and habitats through sound science and active management. The two basic principles of the North American Model of Wildlife Conservation are that fish and wildlife belong to all the people and they are managed in such a way as to sustain healthy populations forever. For more information on the seven pillars of conservation that comprise the North American model, go to: http://www.boone-crockett.org/conservation/conservation_NAM.asp?area=conservation

Shooting, Hunting and American Wildlife –
A PARTNERSHIP

There is a rich history of shooting and hunting in America. This deep love of hunting and shooting by many Americans has also been important to the conservation and management of wildlife in America.

In the early 1900s, Americans became concerned when they saw wildlife disappearing – elk, pronghorn, bighorn sheep, deer, turkeys, geese. Citizens rallied to create an agency that would manage the taking of wildlife and protect their state's natural resources. To fund a fish and wildlife agency, hunting and fishing licenses were created and limits set on what could be harvested. The result was a great success story for the comeback of wildlife species across the country. Hunters and anglers were hailed as conservationists for their willingness to pay for what they were benefiting from. And they were willing to do even more.

In 1937 Congress passed the Federal Aid in Wildlife Restoration Act (also known as the Pittman-Robertson Act after the men that introduced it). The act established an 11% excise tax on sporting arms and ammunition to provide funding for wildlife management, restoration, and research, as well as hunter education. In 1950, the Dingell-Johnson Act was passed to establish a tax on fishing tackle and boats to provide state funding for research and management of game fish. In both cases, hunters, anglers, and shooters supported having their equipment taxed. The majority of funding for state wildlife programs comes from hunting and fishing licenses and fees and from the federal tax on sport hunting and fishing equipment and ammunition.

Another important partnership supported by hunters and anglers has been conservation organizations working to bring back specific species. Members have financially supported such groups as Pheasants Forever, National Wild Turkey Federation, Ducks Unlimited, Rocky Mountain Elk Foundation, Trout Unlimited and other groups to help make sure there are healthy populations of wildlife to enjoy and to hunt.

How much money is raised and how is it used?

The Pittman-Robertson Act and Dingell-Johnson Act collect $700 million each year. Since 1937, hunters, shooters, and anglers have contributed over $10 BILLION for wildlife conservation! License fees (in-state, out-of-state, and lifetime) along with special permits and stamps are also ways that users pay to support fish and wildlife management, restoration, and research. Much of the money raised for game species also benefits non-game species like songbirds. When habitats such as wetlands, forests, and grasslands are protected, ALL wildlife benefit. And you benefit too. If you enjoy to watch birds or photograph wildlife or hike and camp, you are benefiting.

What would happen if there were no hunting, fishing, and shooting?

Hunters, anglers, and shooters have played a significant role in the management and wise use of our natural resources. Regardless of whether or not you choose to actively participate in any of these, you should understand and appreciate the role sportsmen and women play in supporting wildlife conservation.

If there were no hunting, fishing, and shooting, there would be no money to help manage wildlife populations and habitat. This means habitat would not be protected and managed and wildlife populations would not be scientifically studied and managed.

The result – ALL wildlife would be in danger. Without money and agencies and organizations to protect and manage habitats and wildlife, many species of wildlife could not survive.

Great American Wildlife Conservation Success Story

The wild turkey was a common site early in our country's history. Unfortunately, over-hunting by settlers and loss of habitat decreased the numbers of wild turkeys in North America to around 30,000 birds. Thanks to conservation efforts and dollars from Pittman-Robertson and hunting licenses, there are over seven million wild turkeys across North America today.

Everyone benefits from Conservation!!!

The future of wildlife conservation depends on the future of shooting, hunting, and angling. Without these enjoyable activities and the monies raised from licenses and equipment sales, there would be little or no money for conservation efforts in our country.

The future of our nation's wildlife is in the hands of the next generation. So why are you important?

Importance of the
Next Generation

So...if more people hunt, shoot, and fish, more money is raised to protect our wild spaces and our wildlife! That is why it is important that young people learn to enjoy shooting and hunting and become life-long shooters and hunters. When you shoot and hunt, you purchase firearms, ammunition, shooting and hunting equipment, and hunting licenses. A part of each one of your purchases goes back to help protect and manage wildlife for everyone!!

If young people do not get interested and involved in these pastimes, there will be less and less money to manage habitat and wildlife. And there will be less people who care about conservation. Eventually, it will put all wildlife in danger and mean less and less wildlife for everyone to enjoy.

Getting Started
in the shooting sports

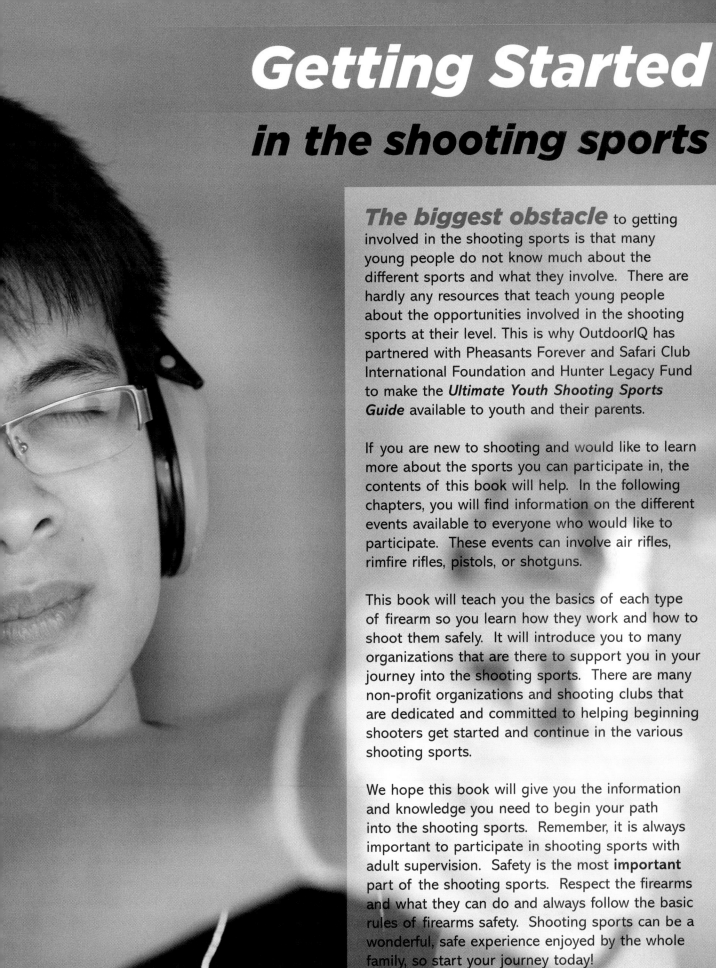

The biggest obstacle to getting involved in the shooting sports is that many young people do not know much about the different sports and what they involve. There are hardly any resources that teach young people about the opportunities involved in the shooting sports at their level. This is why OutdoorIQ has partnered with Pheasants Forever and Safari Club International Foundation and Hunter Legacy Fund to make the *Ultimate Youth Shooting Sports Guide* available to youth and their parents.

If you are new to shooting and would like to learn more about the sports you can participate in, the contents of this book will help. In the following chapters, you will find information on the different events available to everyone who would like to participate. These events can involve air rifles, rimfire rifles, pistols, or shotguns.

This book will teach you the basics of each type of firearm so you learn how they work and how to shoot them safely. It will introduce you to many organizations that are there to support you in your journey into the shooting sports. There are many non-profit organizations and shooting clubs that are dedicated and committed to helping beginning shooters get started and continue in the various shooting sports.

We hope this book will give you the information and knowledge you need to begin your path into the shooting sports. Remember, it is always important to participate in shooting sports with adult supervision. Safety is the most **important** part of the shooting sports. Respect the firearms and what they can do and always follow the basic rules of firearms safety. Shooting sports can be a wonderful, safe experience enjoyed by the whole family, so start your journey today!

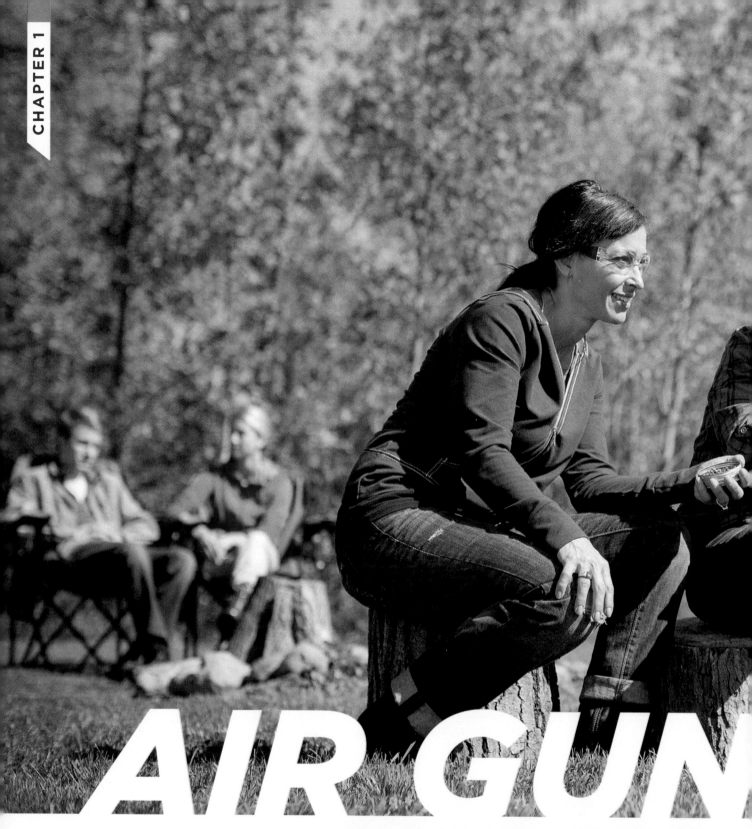

CHAPTER 1

AIR GUN

There are many activities and competitions that young people can participate and enjoy in air gun shooting sports.

PLINKING

Photo credit: Crosman

BB COMPETITIONS

Photo credit: Crosman

SPORTS

POSTAL COMPETITIONS

AIR PISTOL COMPETITIONS

3 POSITION AIR RIFLE

Air guns are a great way to be introduced into the shooting sports. Air guns provide a fun, enjoyable shooting experience because they are quiet and easy to shoot. In this chapter, you will learn about how air guns work, the different types of air guns available, and the various sports involving air guns.

So what is an air gun?

Air gun – a gun that propels a projectile by means of compressed air or gas.

You may think air guns are new, but they are not. Air guns have been around for thousands of years. Maybe not the air guns we know today. The first air guns were used by people many, many years ago. In fact, the first air guns were powered by our lungs! Blowguns were the first air guns that people used. There is evidence they were used even before 125 A.D.

Even the air guns that are familiar to us today date back over 100 years. One of the most famous air guns in history was the air gun that Meriwether Lewis, of the Lewis and Clark Expedition, took on his expedition. The Girandoni air rifle amazed the Native Americans as Lewis demonstrated and shot the gun with no smoke and very little sound. At the time it was introduced, it cost a whopping $2.00!! Here in America, the air gun was made popular when the first "wirestock" Daisy model was introduced in 1888.

Since that first air gun was introduced, air guns have come a long way and have evolved into a fast growing and exciting sport.

Photo credit: Daisy

Today you can shoot air guns that range from the simple BB gun to a high tech, precision air rifle. No matter what you choose to shoot, air guns provide a fun, inexpensive way to enter the world of shooting sports.

Even though you may think that an air gun is not powerful because it uses just air, that is NOT the case! Air guns are powerful, serious firearms and they must be used with care and safety. Even BB guns can be dangerous if they are not used properly and safely. This chapter will teach you the important things you need to know about air guns so you are familiar with all the aspects of air guns and use them safely.

Photo credit: Daisy

Photo credit: Daisy

How do air guns work?

There are several different ways to power an air gun. These can be divided into three broad groups; spring piston, pneumatic, and CO2. It is important you know how the different air guns work because these different methods are used in all types of air guns, from air rifles and air pistols, even to simple BB guns.

Spring Piston

This group of air guns uses cocking a lever or barrel to power the gun. Cocking the lever or barrel causes a spring that is attached to a piston to compress. Once the piston is released, it pushes air out of the barrel. This air pressure shoots the projectile out of the barrel.

Steps involved in cocking and shooting a spring piston air gun:

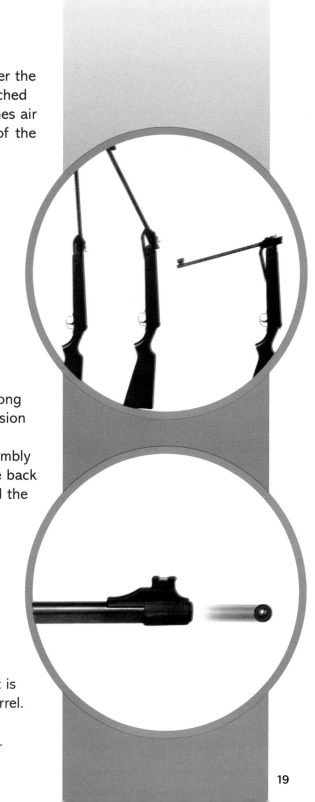

1. Start by making sure your firearm is pointed in a safe direction down range.

2. Keeping the barrel pointed in a safe direction, cock the gun by using the lever or barrel.

3. The cocking action causes the piston to compress the strong spring and pushes the piston to the back of the compression chamber. Once the piston is pushed to the back of the chamber, the piston clicks into a notch in the trigger assembly called the sear. The sear or notch keeps the piston in the back of the chamber and prevents it from moving forward until the trigger is pulled.

4. When the trigger is pulled, it causes the sear to release the piston. This allows the spring to release and push the piston forward in the chamber. As the piston moves quickly forward, it pushes or compresses the air in front of it.

5. The air is pushed through the air transfer port and then into the barrel. This air then pushes the pellet or BB that is in the barrel at a high rate of speed until it leaves the barrel.

Steps #4 and #5 only take a fraction of a second to happen.

Types of Cocking Actions

BARREL BREAKING	UNDER LEVER	SIDE LEVER	TOP LEVER
1	**2**	**3**	**4**

Important Tip: The worst thing you can do to a spring piston air gun is to "dry-fire" it. This means to cock and fire the gun without a pellet in the barrel. This can damage your air gun and affect its accuracy.

Pneumatic

Pneumatic air guns use compressed air to propel a pellet or BB. There are three types of pneumatic air guns.

❶ **Single stroke** – uses a lever to compress air into an air storage chamber by pumping the lever one single time.

❷ **Multi-stroke** – uses a lever to compress air into an air storage chamber by pumping the lever multiple times.

❸ **Pre-charged** – the air storage chamber is filled by using a hand pump or a charged cylinder.

Photo credit: Crosman

Single Stroke

This type is similar to the multi-stroke but only requires one single stroke of the cocking lever to compress the air. This type of air gun is used in 10 meter air gun matches because of its accuracy.

Advantages: The single stroke creates a consistent pressure for good accuracy
Disadvantages: Because it only uses a single stroke, the gun lacks power beyond 10 meters

Multi-stroke

Photo credit: Daisy

This type of pneumatic air gun is commonly referred to as a pump air gun because it uses a pump lever on the gun to force air into an air storage chamber or reservoir. Multi-stroke air guns can be pumped from 2 to 10 strokes to build up the air pressure needed to shoot the pellet or BB out of the barrel. The more pumps, the more air pressure is stored, the faster the muzzle velocity and the further the gun will shoot.

Advantages: Lightweight, compact, and average accuracy
Disadvantages: Takes significant time and effort to get a shot off from the gun, many variables involved which can affect consistent performance

Pre-charged

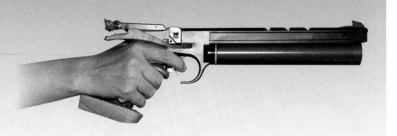

Pre-charged pneumatic or PCP air guns have an air reservoir on the guns that must be filled. The reservoir can be filled by using a hand pump or from a tank, such as a scuba or air tank. The reservoir can hold enough compressed air to shoot up to 500 shots.

This type of gun is the most popular gun used by competition shooters.

Advantages: Very little recoil, very consistent and accurate, takes little effort to load
Disadvantages: More expensive gun, must have a way to charge the air reservoir

Pre-charged air guns must be charged with 3000 psi or pounds per square inch. This is a lot of air pressure. This pressure can be created by hand pumps or compressed air tanks.

Hand pumping – This method uses a hand pump to pump air into the gun, similar to pumping up a bike tire. The hand pump uses the energy from a person to force air into the gun's reservoir. This takes several minutes and requires a lot of strength and power. The pumping begins easy at first, but then becomes more difficult as the reservoir fills with air. Hand pumps work well but take a lot of time and energy.

Tanks – This method uses compressed air in a storage tank, which is transferred to the gun's reservoir using a connection hose. Special gauges allow you to know when the reservoir on the gun is filled. This only takes a couple of seconds but requires special equipment. Charging with compressed air can be very dangerous and should only be done by someone with experience and the correct equipment.

Pressure guage on air rifle

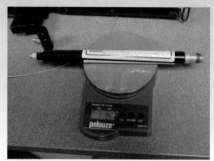
Weighing air cylinder to check fill level

Large compressed air charging system

CO_2

This type of air gun is powered by compressed carbon dioxide (CO2). The gun will use either a 12 gram CO2 cartridge or a larger, refillable CO2 tank. The CO2 is affected by temperature. If the temperature increases or decreases significantly, it can really affect the power and accuracy of the gun.

Advantages: Easy to use and charge, no pressure regulation needed, very affordable guns
Disadvantages: Temperature affects accuracy, cost of cylinders or cartridges

What type of air gun do I need?

This is the question many first time or even experienced shooters ask. It really depends on your experience and what you want to do with the gun. Different types of air guns are designed for different skill levels and events. Let's explore the various types and what each are typically used for.

Beginner Air Guns

BB Guns

BB guns are many times the beginning shooter's first gun. Quick facts about BB guns:

Photo credit: Daisy

- Usually spring piston powered
- Barrel is not rifled, which means the inside of the barrel is smooth
- Shoot BBs which are small, round, metal projectiles
- Less powerful, lightweight, and inexpensive
- Great for learning shooting fundamentals

BB-Pellet Guns

The next step up from BB guns are BB-Pellet guns. There are many advantages to this type of gun for the beginner. Quick facts about BB-Pellet guns:

Photo credit: Daisy

- Usually a pump pneumatic style gun
- Barrel can be smooth or rifled
- As the name implies, it can shoot either BBs or pellets
- More powerful than BB guns, but still inexpensive
- Can be accurate and consistent with practice.

Competition Guns

Photo credit: Daisy

Sporter

This style air gun is usually the entry-level gun for shooters as they begin to shoot in competitions. As young shooters want a gun that is more accurate and capable of being used in various competitions across the nation, the sporter is the air gun they choose. Quick facts about sporter rifles:

Photo credit: Crosman

- Most are pneumatic or CO2
- Single shot
- Very accurate and have several regulations that the gun must follow
- Usually has competitive, higher end sights
- Sporter pistols are also available for pistol competitions
- Costs range from $300 to $800 although some organizations limit the cost of the gun to encourage everyone to participate.

Precision

The precision air guns are the top of the air gun world. These guns look like something out of a science fiction movie. They are high tech, cool looking guns used by shooters who are serious about competition. Facts about precision guns:

- Single shot and extremely accurate
- Type of air gun used in Olympic-style competitions
- Most are pre-charged pneumatic (PCP) powered
- Made to shoot 10 meters
- Precision pistols are also available
- Costs range from $800 to $3000

Hunting Guns

There are more and more air guns being designed specifically for hunting. Using an air gun is a fun and a quiet way to hunt small game such as squirrels. There are many hunting air guns on the market to choose from. Facts about hunting guns:

Photo credit: Daisy

Photo credit: Crosman

- Usually shoot pellets at very high velocity or speed
- Very accurate
- Many use a telescopic sight (scope) for added accuracy at longer distances
- Most common calibers are .177 and .22
- Costs range from $150 to $800

Photo credit: Crosman

What do air guns shoot?

What is a projectile?

· · · · · · · · · · · ·

A projectile is any object projected into space by the exertion of a force.

Different air guns shoot different projectiles. The most common types of projectiles or ammunition that air guns use are BBs and pellets.

Let's learn more about these different types of projectiles or ammo....

BBs

BBs got their name from round BB shot, which was the size of shotgun shot put into shotgun shells. BB shot is 0.180 inches in diameter and is made of lead. These first BBs were not very consistent in size and shape.

No matter if they are silver, gold, or copper color, BBs are made of steel. BBs are now 0.177 inches or 4.5 mm in diameter. **Because they are made of steel, today's BBs are much harder and can ricochet when they hit a hard surface.**

BB FACTS
BBs are not as aerodynamic as other projectiles, so they are not as accurate.
BBs are mainly used for plinking and recreational shooting.
BBs are still a dangerous projectile and should always be shot with adult supervision.

Pellets

Pellets are projectiles that are usually made of lead. However, there are lead-free pellets that can be used as an alternative. All pellets have a diabolo shape.

DIABOLO – an hour-glass shaped object that was a common toy played with two sticks and a string.

The pellet has a tip that tapers down to a narrow waist and then flares out again into a hollow base. This shape does two things for the pellet.

1. It adds stability to the flight of the pellet. This means it makes the pellet fly straighter and more accurately. Look at the shape of a pellet and a badminton "birdie" or shuttlecock. They have the same basic shape. The shape of a badminton "birdie" helps it fly straight and true, just like the pellet.

2. This wide hollow base also flares out when air pushes the pellet. The soft flare actually molds to the barrel so that as the air is released behind it, the air cannot escape around the pellet. The air then pushes the pellet down the barrel at a high speed. The soft flare or "skirt" of the pellet interacts with the riflings or grooves inside of the barrel to spin the pellet and this increases the accuracy and shooting distance.

Sizes and Types of Pellets

Pellets are sized by the diameter of the widest part of the pellet. This size is usually measured in thousandths of an inch. This measurement is known as a caliber. The most common size of pellet is .177 caliber. The metric measurement for this size of pellet is 4.5 mm. Other sizes of pellets include 0.20 and 0.22 calibers.

4 Basic Pellet Types

WADCUTTER	ROUND NOSE OR DOMED	POINTED	HOLLOW POINT

WADCUTTER

This type of pellet has a flat tip or head.

FACTS:

- Commonly used in target shooting because it makes a clean hole in the target.
- Accurate up to 10-20 yards.
- Loses accuracy beyond 20 yards because the flat head is affected by the wind.

ROUND NOSE OR DOMED

This pellet has a rounded head or a dome shape.

FACTS:

- Very aerodynamic making them a great all-around pellet for shooting.
- Very accurate at long distances.
- Used in high powered air rifles because of their aerodynamics.
- Effective for hunting because it has good speed, impact, and accuracy.

POINTED

This pellet has a pointed head.

FACTS:

- Designed for good penetration in light or medium powered air guns.

HOLLOW POINT

This pellet has a hollow head.

FACTS:

- Designed to expand when they hit the target and have maximum impact.
- Requires a medium or high powered air gun to make it expand.
- Good choice for hunting at close range because they do not penetrate the target very deep.
- Not as accurate at long distances because the hollow tip catches the air.

So, how fast does an air gun shoot?

This is a question that many shooters ask when they want to know how fast a given gun can shoot. Now let's learn some gun science. We determine how fast a gun shoots by measuring its velocity, or sometimes referred to as speed. So...what is velocity?

$$V = \frac{distance}{time}$$

Velocity – how far an object travels in a given unit of time.

$$Velocity = \frac{distance}{time}$$

The most common measure of velocity is miles per hour. We often measure a car's velocity or speed in the distance unit of miles and the time unit of hours to calculate the mile per hour or mph. We all know the normal speed limit in most places is 55 mph. How does that compare to how fast a gun shoots?

First, we have to talk about the units we used when we measure the velocity or speed of a gun. The units we use are feet per second (fps). This is how many feet a projectile can travel in one second and is measured at the time the projectile leaves the barrel.

For example, if an air gun shoots a pellet at 500 fps, that means the pellet will travel 500 feet in a single second.

How do feet per second compare to miles per hour? Let's explore and compare the speed of some things you may know.

Car traveling at 55 mph = 80 fps

Pitcher throwing at 95 mph = 139 fps

Pellet Rifle shooting at 500 fps = 340 mph

Comparing the Speed of Different Guns

Now that you understand how the speed of air guns is measured and how they compare with miles per hour, let's look at how the different types of air guns compare.

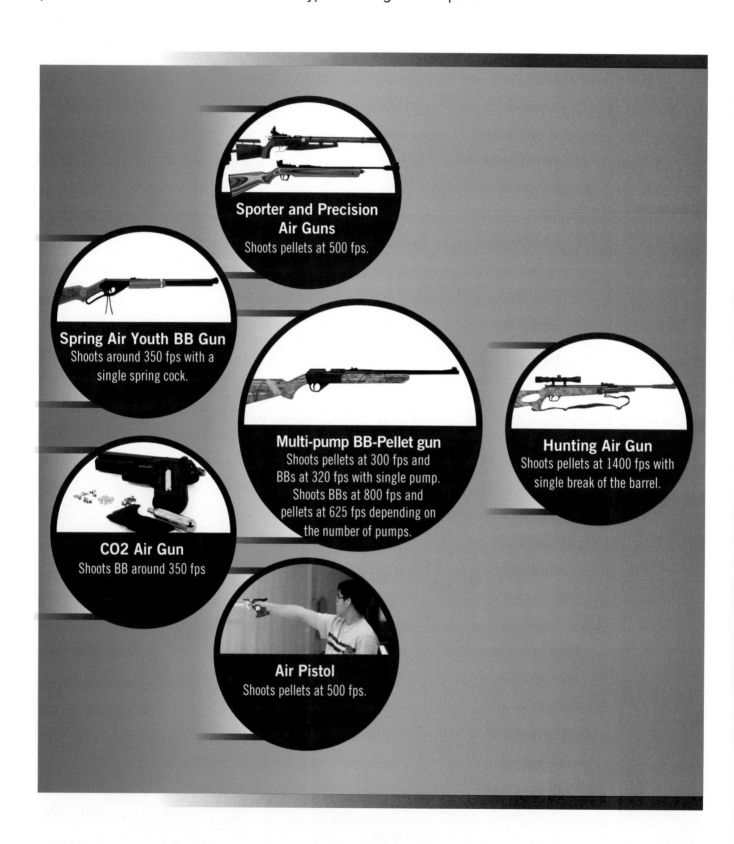

Sporter and Precision Air Guns
Shoots pellets at 500 fps.

Spring Air Youth BB Gun
Shoots around 350 fps with a single spring cock.

Multi-pump BB-Pellet gun
Shoots pellets at 300 fps and BBs at 320 fps with single pump. Shoots BBs at 800 fps and pellets at 625 fps depending on the number of pumps.

Hunting Air Gun
Shoots pellets at 1400 fps with single break of the barrel.

CO2 Air Gun
Shoots BB around 350 fps

Air Pistol
Shoots pellets at 500 fps.

What about the speeds of other firearms?

Most firearms and archery equipment measure speeds in feet per second as well. We now know how fast different air guns can shoot, but how does that compare to other firearms or even bows?

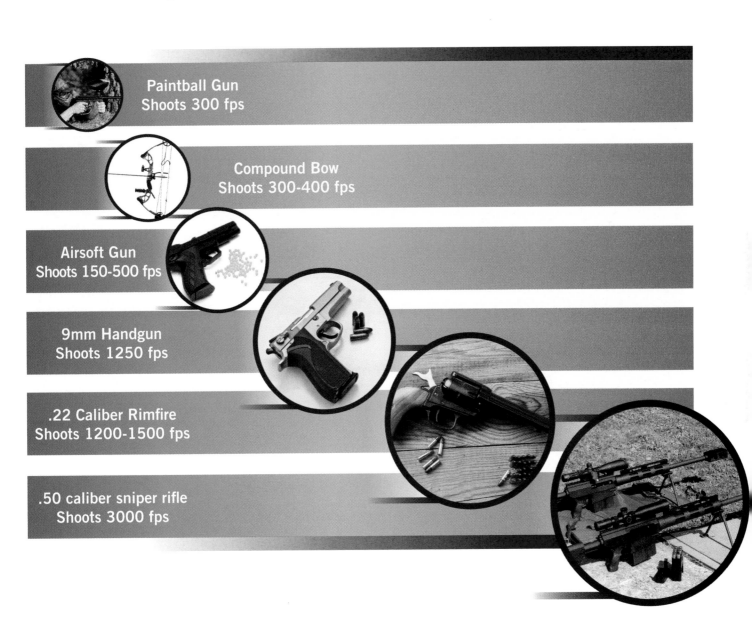

Paintball Gun
Shoots 300 fps

Compound Bow
Shoots 300-400 fps

Airsoft Gun
Shoots 150-500 fps

9mm Handgun
Shoots 1250 fps

.22 Caliber Rimfire
Shoots 1200-1500 fps

.50 caliber sniper rifle
Shoots 3000 fps

Warning: A study looked at how fast a projectile has to travel to penetrate human skin. The study found it only takes between 290 to 365 fps for a projectile to penetrate your skin!! If you look at the speeds of all of the air guns in this chapter, ALL of them have the speed and power to penetrate human skin!!
ONLY SHOOT AIR GUNS OR ANY FIREARM WITH ADULT SUPERVISION!!!

Safely Using and Shooting Your Air Gun

Loading an Air Gun

Because there are so many different types of air guns, there are also many different ways they can be loaded. Air guns use three basic methods to load a projectile.

Hopper – this is a storage chamber to hold the projectiles, usually BBs, and the projectile is loaded one at a time when the gun is cocked or the bolt is activated.

Most BB guns use a hopper. You just pour or place the BBs into the hopper through an opening on the side of the gun or barrel.

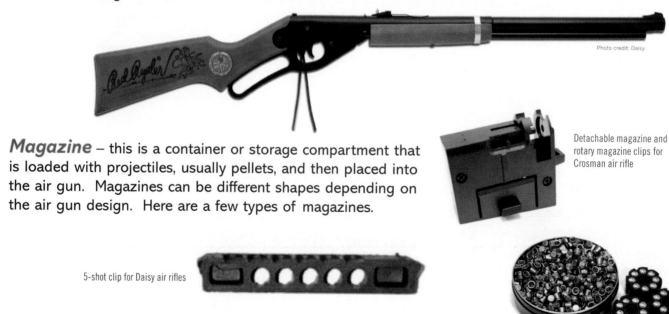

Photo credit: Daisy

Magazine – this is a container or storage compartment that is loaded with projectiles, usually pellets, and then placed into the air gun. Magazines can be different shapes depending on the air gun design. Here are a few types of magazines.

Detachable magazine and rotary magazine clips for Crosman air rifle

5-shot clip for Daisy air rifles

Single shot – this is what the name says - you load one, single shot at a time. To load a single shot air gun, you place a single pellet into the chamber. Many competition air guns are single shot air guns.

Many hunting air rifles are single shots.

Most precision and sporter air rifles are single shots.

Shooting Your Air Gun

To safely shoot your air gun, you must know how to aim your gun correctly. To aim an air gun you must use a sight. The sight is what you look at or through while you aim at your target. As you look at the sight and the target, that is called the "sight picture." Good shooters always use the same sight picture each time they aim and shoot.

Three common types of sights.

Classic iron sights – These are the most common type of sight and are sometimes called open sights. This type of sight has a rear sight that is shaped like a "V" and a front sight that is a single bead or post. The sight picture should have the front post lined up in the middle of the rear sight and even at the top, with the bull's eye at the top of the center post.

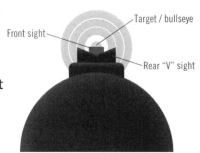

Advantages: Easy to use, very simple parts
Disadvantages: Hard to see the target at long ranges

Aperture or peep sights – These are used by many target shooters. The front sight is similar to open sights, but the rear sight is a disc with a small hole in the center (aperture or peep). The shooter's eye is placed close to this disc and the eye sees the front post and target through the hole. The sight picture usually places the top of the front post slightly below the bull's eye of the target.

Advantages: Limits the sight picture, good to use for irregular shaped targets
Disadvantages: Shooter must get their eye very close to the aperture, hard to sight on black targets.

Telescopic sights or scope – These sights use magnification lenses with crosshair or reticule. The crosshair of the telescopic sight is lined up on the center of the target to make the sight picture.

Advantages: Magnifies the target, useful at longer distances, easier to shoot accurately
Disadvantages: Adds weight to the gun, making it more difficult to handle.

Practicing with your Air Gun

Like any sport, you only get better by practicing. Practicing your shooting skills can make you a better shooter. You must shoot as much as you can to train your eyes and muscles to do the same thing each time you shoot. Doing something over and over develops what is called "muscle memory." There are many sports that involve muscle memory. Muscle memory allows you to do something the same way every time without even thinking about it. It is like a habit.

You can actually practice and develop muscle memory without even shooting the gun. You can do this by sighting your gun at the target and "dry firing" your gun. This means pulling the trigger without having any projectile in the chamber of the gun and having the gun cocked or charged. As mentioned earlier, it is important you do not dry fire a spring piston air gun!

Aiming the gun at the target and pulling the trigger over and over, helps develop the muscle memory and allows you to do all of the important steps to aiming and shooting without actually shooting the gun.

Shooting for Real

You will eventually want to actually shoot a projectile at a target. When you practice with actual ammunition, you will do the same exact process as you did when you dry fire practiced. The difference, now, is that you are shooting the projectile down range. Because you are shooting a loaded gun, you must always follow the basic rules of firearm safety and shoot with adult supervision.

Rules of Firearm Safety

✓ Always keep the gun unloaded until it is ready to be shot.
✓ Always point the muzzle of the gun in a safe direction.
✓ Be sure of your target and what is beyond the target.

✓ Don't rely on your gun's safety.
✓ Don't put your finger on the trigger until you are ready to shoot.
✓ Wear eye and ear protection.
✓ Use the correct ammunition for your gun.

Targets

It is very important that the air gun is shot into a safe backstop or target. Pellets and BBs can travel a good distance and can harm someone they strike. Therefore, you must always be sure the area beyond or behind the target is clear of people, pets, or buildings. Targets should be made of a soft material or a trap that catches the BB or pellet. This will prevent the BB or pellet from ricocheting off a hard surface and possibly coming back toward the shooter or any person nearby.

Scoring Targets

Most targets have various numbers of scoring rings depending on the type of event or target. No matter the number of scoring rings, the scoring is done the same way.
Here is how it works:

- The target rings are scored 10 for the center ring, then decrease by 1 as you move away from the center of the target.
- If the hole the projectile makes, touches any part of the ring on the target it is scored with that number of points.

Example:
Shot #1 is touching the 10 ring only and is scored a 10. Shot #2 is just touching the 8 ring, so it is scored an 8.

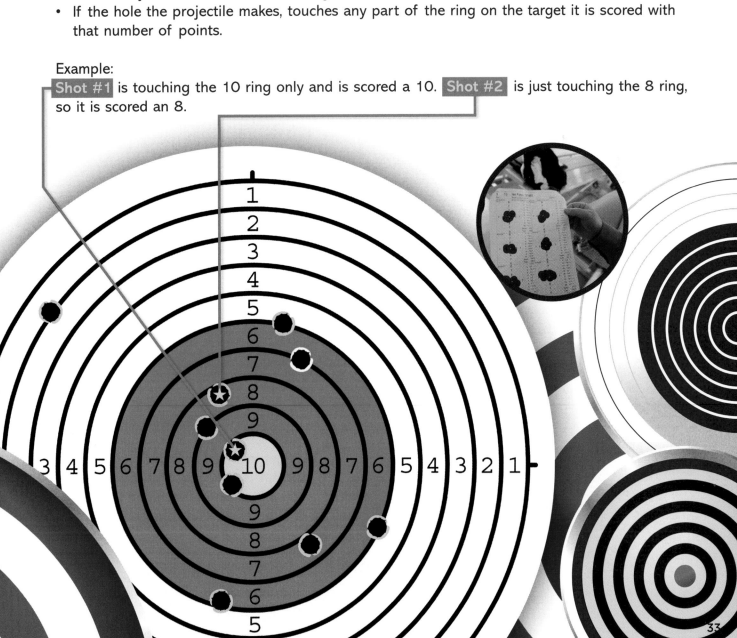

Photo credit: Daisy

Air Gun Activities and Shooting Sports

Plinking

Plinking is an activity that can be enjoyed by the whole family. Plinking is where shooters have fun and shoot a variety of targets.

Many shooters begin plinking by shooting cans or plastic bottles. Plinking can also involve shooting paper targets, metal targets or even homemade targets like balloons. Everyone can enjoy plinking, from beginner to expert shooters.

Whenever you plink, you must be sure to have a good backstop or a target that catches the projectiles. One common target that is safe to shoot into is a pellet trap. This target has an angled back that directs the pellet down into a space where it is trapped.

Photo credit: Crosman

Safety Reminder: Always be sure of your target and what is beyond.

BB Competitions

Many beginning shooters start with BB gun competitions. Most of these competitions are held in a club setting and are planned and organized by shooting clubs or organizations. The rules of BB gun competitions vary depending on the organization running the competition.

To get started with this type of competition, check out these organizations:

4-H Shooting Sports

Photo credit: Daisy

When you think of 4-H, you may not think of shooting sports but there are many opportunities for young people to get involved in shooting by finding a local 4-H shooting club. Some states run a 5-meter BB gun competition, similar to a 5-meter air rifle competition.

These 4-H competitions can be enjoyed by shooting on a team or individually. Shooters shoot BBs from a distance of

5-meters. These competitions can involve shooting from standing, sitting, kneeling, and prone (lying on your stomach) positions.

Shooters shoot a fixed number of shots from each position and the total scores are added. In some competitions, shooters must take a written safety exam and that score is added to their shooting score. This makes sure shooters know the safety rules and will be safe on the range. Find out more about 4-H shooting sports at www.4-hshootingsports.org

Boy Scouts

Boy scouts provide opportunities for young people to begin their shooting journey by teaching young shooters the basics of shooting and allowing them to shoot BB gun activities and competitions. Some boy scout troops hold different shooting games and events. Some have fun shooting a game of tic tac toe using rows of balloons.

Others hold 'Bikathlons,' a competition modeled after the Olympic biathlon where competitors cross country ski and shoot rifles. The bikathlon has shooters ride bikes on an off-road course, get off their bikes at different target locations and shoot at the targets.

Daisy National BB Gun Championship Match

Daisy is known as the company which popularized the BB gun in the late 1880s. Today, Daisy hosts the Daisy National BB Gun Championship Match or Daisy Nationals, which is the national match for Daisy-sponsored 5-meter BB gun marksmanship programs held around the country.

Only those teams that come in first, second or third place at a sanctioned state match will qualify to attend and compete in the Daisy Nationals.

You can be part of a 5-meter BB gun team by joining an organization that shoots 5-meter BB gun competitions such as 4-H, the American Legion, Royal Rangers, Boy Scouts, as well as other groups that train and sponsor shooting teams.

At the nationals, about 450 young people ages 8 to 15 compete using the single-shot BB gun called the Daisy AVANTI Champion, Model 499. They shoot in four positions and take a safety exam. The highest scoring teams and individuals are recognized with awards. You can find out more about the Daisy BB Gun Nationals at www.daisy.com/daisynationals.

3-Position Air Rifle Competitions

This shooting competition is exactly what the name says. Shooters shoot at a target at 10 meters while shooting in three different positions.

STANDING   KNEELING   PRONE

Each shooter shoots a set of shots from each position. The type of match is determined by the number of shots that are shot from each position. Each set of shots must be shot in a given time limit.

3 x 10 Course of Fire

Prone: 10 shots in 10 minutes
Standing: 10 shots in 15 minutes
Kneeling: 10 shots in 10 minutes

3 x 20 Course of Fire

Prone: 20 shots in 20 minutes
Standing: 20 shots in 25 minutes
Kneeling: 20 shots in 20 minutes

Shooters shoot the positions in that exact order. Prone first, followed by standing, and finish with kneeling. Each round is scored and the total score is calculated. Scoring can be done manually by a person or by an electronic scoring system.

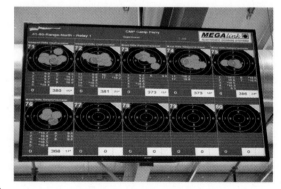

Different Classes of 3-Position Air Rifle

There are two classes of 3-position air rifle competitions. These classes are based on the equipment being used. The two classes are Sporter and Precision.

Sporter Class

- Low cost, entry-level rifle
- Must be .177 caliber
- Pneumatic, spring air, compressed air or CO2 powered rifles
- Must be 600 fps or less
- Shooters wear regular clothing

Precision Class

- Higher cost, specialized rifle
- Must be .177 caliber
- Pneumatic, spring air, compressed air or CO2 powered rifles
- Must be 600 fps or less
- Shooters wear specialized shooting clothing

Progressive-Position Pistol (PPP) Competitions

This program is a partnership between USA Shooting and the National Rifle Association (NRA). This shooting competition is intended to introduce young shooters to competitive shooting and is the beginning of a shooter's journey into the Junior Olympic pistol competitions. The distance of the competitions is 10 meters. This competition uses air pistols of .177 caliber and spring air, compressed air or CO2 powered. Pistols can only have open sights.

Beginner Categories of PPP

Basic Supported

Facts about Basic Supported

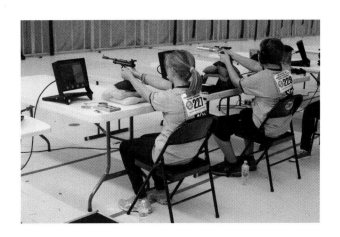

- Open to shooters 13 and under
- Shooter can be seated or stand
- Use 1 or 2 hand grip
- Grip and hands may be rested on a firm support
- Shoot 40 shots

Standing Supported

Facts about Standing Supported

- Open to shooters 15 and under
- Shooter must stand
- Use 1 hand grip
- Can be supported by T-stand or counterbalance
- Shoot 40 shots

Sub-junior International Standing

Facts about International Standing

- Open to shooters up to 20 years of age.
- Shooter must stand
- Use 1 hand grip with no support
- This is the Olympic Air Pistol event to develop Olympic pistol athletes.
- The Olympic Air Pistol event is 60 shots for men and 40 shots for women.

Postal Competitions

Some organizations hold 'postal' competitions. The name really explains how the competition works.

How Does it Work???

Many different organizations sponsor postal competitions. The competing shooters purchase official targets from the sponsoring organization. Individuals or teams shoot the competition at their range or location. An important part of this type of competition is honesty and integrity of shooters and their teams because the targets are shot at their own range. Clubs then mail their targets to the organization and the organization scores them. This allows shooters to compete against other shooters from across the nation without having to travel. A big advantage is that teams can compete in postal competitions and qualify for larger state or national competitions.

Postal competitions can involve BB or pellet guns. What shooting events are held with postal competitions???

- 5-meter BB Gun
- 3-Position air rifle
- 3-Position air pistol

CHAPTER 2

SMALL

There are activities and competitions that young people can participate and enjoy in the smallbore shooting sports.

RIMFIRE SPORTER COMPETITION

Photo credit: CMP

RIMFIRE CHALLENGE

Photo credit: National Shooting Sports Foundation

BORE

3-POSITION SMALLBORE RIFLE

SMALLBORE PISTOL COMPETITIONS

POSTAL COMPETITIONS

Photo credit: USA Shooting Sports

Photo credit: USA Shooting Sports

What is a smallbore?

Smallbore rifles and handguns are sometimes referred to as 22s because they are usually .22 caliber. Smallbore shooting in the United States began in 1919 when Savage and Winchester introduced .22 caliber target rifles. It was from this beginning that the modern smallbore shooting sports originated.

The .22 caliber is the most popular firearm worldwide because of:
*   affordability of smallbore firearms
*   inexpensive ammunition
*   reduced sound or noise
*   minimal recoil

This makes the .22 a great starter firearm for beginning shooters.

There are two basic types of ammunition that rifles use. There are centerfire and rimfire ammunition. For rifle cartridges to fire, a primer is struck by a firing pin of the firearm. When this happens, the primer ignites the powder in the cartridge, which then propels the bullet out the barrel. Centerfire cartridges have the primer in the center of the cartridge.

The ammunition or cartridge used in smallbore firearms is called a rimfire cartridge. The term rimfire is exactly what it implies. The primer is on the rim of the cartridge and fires when it is struck on the rim by the firearm's firing pin.

Science of Shooting

What is recoil???
Recoil is the backward motion or momentum of the firearm when it is shot or discharged. This is a result of Newton's Third Law of Motion. For every action there is an equal reaction.

The motion of the bullet and gases leaving the barrel is equaled by the motion of the firearm in the opposite direction against the shooter. Sometimes this is called the "kick" of the firearm.

Centerfire Cartridge

Rimfire Cartridge

Facts about .22 caliber ammunition:

- The .22 refers to the caliber of the projectile.
- Very accurate up to 150 yards.
- Customized .22 rifles can be accurate up to 300 yards.
- Has a range of 1½ miles!!!

Safety Reminder: Although the .22 round is small, it still is a very dangerous bullet and must always be shot safely and taken very seriously.

Caliber:

the size or diameter of the projectile usually measured in inches.

.22 caliber = 0.22 inches in diameter

If measured in metric it would be 5.56 mm.

Types of .22 Ammunition

.22 Long Rifle or .22LR

- The most common type of .22 ammo used.
- Travels at 1200-1400 fps.
- Accurate to 100-200 yards.
- Approximately a 40 gram bullet.
- Bullets can be hollow point, solid point, or copper plated.
- Bullets usually made of lead.
- The .22 LR is ranked #1 worldwide with more than 2 billion rounds made each year!

Solid Point   Hollow Point

.22 Short

- Same caliber as .22LR but much smaller casing.
- Approximately 29 gram bullet with less powder.
- Travels 1000 fps.
- Used mainly for short range.
- Not used for competition.

.22 Shot shell

- Same size casing as a .22LR, but instead of a lead bullet, it contains small shot like a shotgun.
- Contains 31 grams of #12 shot.
- Travels at 1000 fps.
- Used for pest control at short ranges.

Types of Smallbore Rifles

There are several types of smallbore rifles. These rifles are grouped by the type of action. The action is the way the gun loads, locks, and removes the cartridge from the gun.

Bolt action

A bolt action rifle works by manually opening and closing a bolt at the breech of the gun. The bolt is a mechanism with a handle that pushes a cartridge into the barrel and then pulls the cartridge out of the barrel. The bolt also contains the firing pin and cocks the firing pin when it is opened and closed. The bolt is usually on the right side of the rifle, unless the gun is made for a left-handed shooter, then it is on the left side. Bolt action rifles can be fed by hand as a single shot, or by a multiple shot magazine.

Martini and Lever action

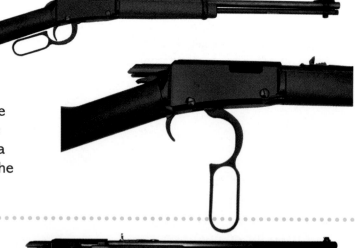

These two actions are very similar and use a lever that is located around or near the trigger guard area. When the lever is pulled down or away from the trigger guard, the cartridge in the chamber is removed. When the lever is pushed back toward the trigger guard, a new cartridge is loaded into the chamber and the gun is cocked.

Pump(slide) action

This action works by sliding the foregrip of the rifle back toward the shooter to remove the cartridge from the magazine. The foregrip is then slid back away from the shooter to load a new cartridge and cock the rifle. The magazine in pump actions is usually an internal, tube magazine.

Semi-automatic or Semi-auto action

This action must have a cartridge in the magazine to load the rifle. The action or bolt of the rifle is pulled back manually to load the cartridge and cock the rifle. The action is called semi-automatic because when the loaded cartridge is shot, the recoil of the rifle being shot automatically moves the action back and the spent cartridge is automatically removed and a new cartridge is loaded, making the rifle cocked and ready to shoot again. This allows the rifle to be shot each time the trigger is pulled as long as there are cartridges in the magazine.

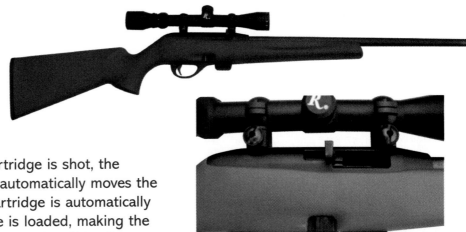

Break or Hinge action

This action works by breaking the rifle open to show the breech of the rifle. The rifle can only shoot one shot at a time because it must be loaded by hand for each shot.
The rifle is usually cocked by pulling back the hammer.

Parts of a Rifle

Parts of a lever action rifle:

REAR SIGHT

HAMMER

BOLT

FOREGRIP

BARREL

FRONT SIGHT

STOCK

TRIGGER GUARD

MAGAZINE TUBE

BORE

TRIGGER

LEVER

Parts of a semi-automatic rifle:

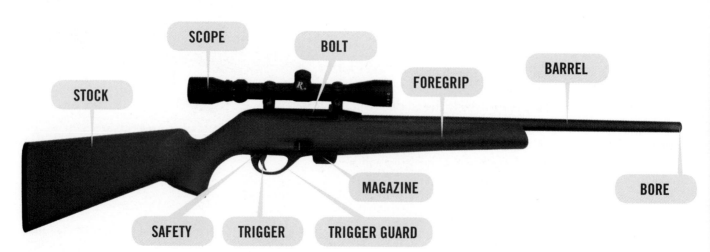

SCOPE

BOLT

FOREGRIP

BARREL

STOCK

MAGAZINE

BORE

SAFETY

TRIGGER

TRIGGER GUARD

Types of Smallbore Handguns

Handguns are firearms that are shot using one or both hands. Handguns are either revolvers or pistols. Let's find out more about these types of handguns.

Revolver

This handgun has a cylinder that revolves and holds multiple cartridges. Most revolvers have cylinders with 5 to 6 chambers. As the revolver is shot, the cylinder rotates to allow another cartridge to be fired.

There are two types of revolvers:

Single action – This revolver is only cocked by pulling back the hammer.

Double action – This revolver can be cocked by either pulling the hammer back or by pulling the trigger. Since it can be cocked and fired by two different ways, it is called a double action.

Revolver

Pistols

Pistols are handguns that have a single barrel and either hold one cartridge at a time or have a magazine that holds several cartridges. Pistols are classified as either semi-automatic or single shot.

Semi-automatic – This pistol has a single barrel with a magazine that holds the cartridges. This pistol must be cocked and loaded by pulling back the slide, which is the top part of the firearm above the grip. Once loaded and cocked, the gun will shoot and load itself by the force of the round going off. This means the gun will shoot each time the trigger is pulled

Single shot – This pistol only holds one round at a time. That round must be fired and removed by hand each time the pistol is shot. This is a common type of pistol used in competitions.

Semi-automatic pistol with clip

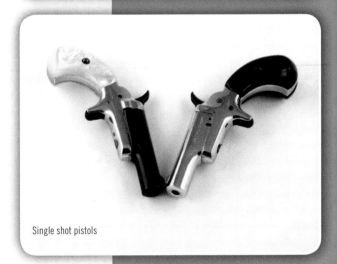
Single shot pistols

Parts of a Handgun

Parts of a revolver

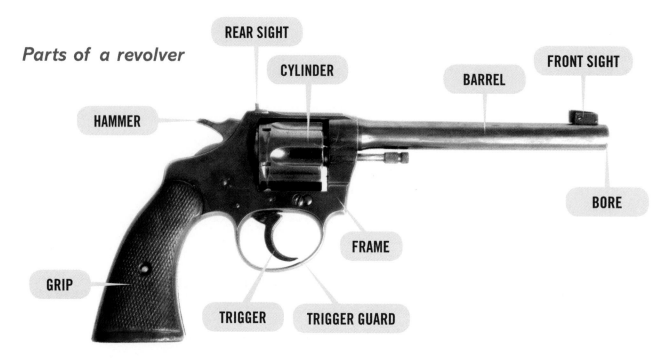

REAR SIGHT

CYLINDER

BARREL

FRONT SIGHT

HAMMER

BORE

GRIP

FRAME

TRIGGER

TRIGGER GUARD

Parts of a semi-automatic pistol

FRONT SIGHT

BARREL

SLIDE

REAR SIGHT

HAMMER

SAFETY

FRAME

MAGAZINE RELEASE

TRIGGER

TRIGGER GUARD

GRIP

MAGAZINE / CLIP

Shooting and Practicing

To be the most accurate shooter you can be takes a lot of practice. When you practice with smallbore firearms, you must be very careful and understand what the firearm and bullets are capable of and how far they can travel. Remember, .22 caliber bullets are accurate to 100-150 yards but can travel MUCH FURTHER, over a mile!

Safety Reminder: Whenever you shoot and practice with a smallbore firearm, you must always have adult supervision and must be sure you are shooting in a safe direction and be aware of what is BEYOND your target.

Shooting Ranges

The safest place to practice your shooting is at professionally designed shooting ranges. These ranges can be indoors or outdoors.

Outdoor Ranges – these ranges use a large backstop usually made from dirt to stop and trap the bullets. It is also important that the backstop does not contain rocks or other hard objects. This will prevent ricochets. Ricochets are when a bullet hits a hard surface and then travels in another unsafe direction. Ricochets can be very dangerous!!

Indoor Ranges – these ranges are probably the safest and best place to practice and shoot. Professional indoor ranges are designed for maximum safety.

Targets

Once you have a safe range at which to shoot, you can have some fun with different types of targets as you practice.

- **Paper targets** – the most common and inexpensive targets

- **Spinning targets** – these targets spin when they are shot.

- **Resetting plate targets** – these targets are made of metal plates that fall down or away when they are hit, but then are reset when another plate is shot.

- **Movable targets** – these targets are free moving targets that move when they are shot.

Stationary clay target

Resetting steel plate target

Stationary steel plate target

Safety Reminder: Whatever target you decide to use, you MUST always use the target in front of a range backstop to be sure the bullets do not travel past the targets!! Also, you should always shoot and practice with adult supervision!!

Rimfire or Smallbore Shooting Sports Events

Rimfire Sporter Competition

Rimfire Sporter is a shooting sports activity that the Civilian Marksmanship Program introduced in 2002 after four years of testing this concept in CMP Rimfire Sporter rifle clinics. Any gun enthusiast or hunter can shoot Rimfire Sporter because it uses smallbore sporter rifles that many of them already own. You do not have to buy expensive target gear to shoot Rimfire Sporter. The Rimfire Sporter course of fire is designed so that every shooter who understands basic gun safety and rifle marksmanship can shoot. Rimfire Sporter is uniquely challenging—it tests shooters' skills in three different firing positions, at two different ranges, in both precision and rapid-fire shooting.

Rimfire Sporter stresses fun, accessibility, and practical marksmanship skills. It is a great game for shooters who want a target event that does not require expensive match-conditioned rifles or gear. It is ideal for hunters who recognize that practicing rimfire rifle shooting throughout the year will make them more skilled marksmen when they pursue game. Rimfire Sporter can be a way to introduce youth and adults to the excitement and fascinating challenges of rifle target shooting. And most importantly, Rimfire Sporter is perfect for the shooter who enjoys going out to the range to have a relaxed competition with friends.

The CMP Rimfire Sporter Rifle Match gives shooters a recreation-oriented competition that allows them to use their rimfire sporters (plinking and small game rifles) on the range. To shoot this match, all you need is a rifle and ammo. Special competition gear is not required or permitted. Competitors use standard, sporter-type rimfire rifles that can weigh no more than 7.5 pounds with sights. Rifles may be manually operated or semi-automatic. Shooters with manually-operated actions are given extra time in rapid-fire.

Photo credits: CMP

Course of Fire for Different Stages:

Stage	Distance	Type of Fire	Firing Position	Number of Shots	Time Limit
Sighters	50 yds.	Slow	Any, a rest may be used	Unlimited	10 min.
1	50 yds.	Slow	Prone	10	10 min.
2	50 yds.	Rapid	Prone	10, fired in 2 series of 5	Semi-auto-25 sec. Manual-30 sec.
3	50 yds.	Slow	Sitting or Kneeling	10	10 min.
4	50 yds.	Rapid	Sitting or Kneeling	10, fired in 2 series of 5	Semi-auto-25 sec. Manual-30 sec.
5	25 yds.	Slow	Standing	10	10 min
6	25 yds.	Rapid	Standing	10, fired in 2 series of 5	Semi-auto-25 sec. Manual-30 sec.

National Shooting Sports Foundation (NSSF) Rimfire Challenge

The NSSF Rimfire Challenge is a .22 rifle and pistol program created to introduce new people to the shooting sports and provide a pathway to shooting competition. The NSSF Rimfire Challenge can provide individuals or families with a fun and exciting first-time shooting experience. The goals of the Rimfire Challenge include the following:

Photo credit: National Shooting Sports Foundation

- Teach SAFE, responsible handling and use of firearms.
- Introduce new shooters to competitive shooting in a safe, fun, and supportive environment.
- Provide a lifetime sport that families can enjoy together.

The NSSF Rimfire Challenge is a family-friendly activity designed to teach new shooters how to get started in competitive shooting. The program's focus is having FUN while being SAFE on the range. The event fees for Registered Matches are to be kept at $50 to $60 per event. Participation is open to all safe and responsible individuals who can legally own, possess, or handle a firearm in the location of the competition or event.

There are two divisions for the Rimfire Challenge events. They include:
1. **Open Division** – Any firearm (pistol, revolver, or rifle) with scopes, optical sights, light- gathering scopes, battery-powered optics, lasers, compensator, or muzzle brake
2. **Limited Division** – Firearms with iron sights, adjustable sights, and fiber optics are allowed. Firearms with electronic sights, compensators, muzzle breaks, or barrel weights are not allowed in this division.

There are several different courses of fire for this event. All of the courses of fire involve shooting steel plates of various sizes in a timed event. The plates are arranged in different ways depending on the course of fire. To see more information about the different courses of fire for the Rimfire Challenge, visit www.nssf.org/Rimfire/files/CoursesOfFire.pdf.

3-Position Smallbore Rifle Competition

This competition is similar to the 3-position air rifle competitions explained in the air rifle chapter. Shooters shoot from kneeling, standing, and prone positions. There are different course of fire and rules depending on the sponsor of the competitions. The most common sponsors of 3-position smallbore rifle events include the National Rifle Association (NRA), USA Shooting, and 4-H Shooting Sports.

Although there are precision 3-position smallbore rifle competitions, such as Olympic events that use specialized precision rifles, many competitions allow any smallbore rifle. There are different classes based on the types of sights being used or different types of rifles.

Smallbore Pistol Competitions

Smallbore pistol competitions involve events at either 25 meters or 50 meters. Any smallbore pistol that shoots .22 caliber long rifle rimfire ammunition can be used in the competitions, as long as it follows the specifications in the rules. Only open sights are allowable and there are specific measurements and weights the pistols must follow. The specific rules for the smallbore pistol competitions for USA Shootings can be found at http://www.usashooting.org/library/ Rulebooks/2014/USAS_Pistol_2014.pdf.

Depending on the actual event, competitions can involve precision stages, rapid fire stages, or both. Precision stages allows shooters to shoot a given number of shots in a given time period. Rapid fire stages require shooters to shoot five-shot-series of shots in varying number of seconds, usually from 4 to 150 seconds. The stages typically involve 2 to 6 five-shot-series. These competitions are fast-paced and exciting.

Scholastic Pistol Program (SPP)

The Scholastic Shooting Sports Foundation (SSSF) offers a pistol shooting program for youth speed shooting on steel targets. The program is for kids from 12 years old through college and offers the opportunity to safely participate in an exciting team-based sport. The program uses both smallbore or rimfire pistols, as well as centerfire pistols. Shooters shoot rectangular and circular steel plates in timed events. To find out more about SPP go to http://sssfonline.org/scholastic-pistol-program-spp/.

Postal Matches

Like air rifle, smallbore also has postal competitions. Individuals and club teams can compete in postal competitions by shooting a specific smallbore competition recognized by the organization that is sponsoring the competition. The rules of the given competition are followed and the individual or team shoots the competition at their own location and the targets are mailed to the sponsoring organization to be officially scored. The NRA and 4-H Shooting Sports sponsor and organize postal matches for smallbore rifle competitions. Check out the NRA and 4-H Shooting Sports to find out more about their postal matches.

Ways to get started in Smallbore Shooting Sports

If you are totally new to shooting smallbore firearms, the best place to begin is a local shooting range. These ranges have special classes to teach new shooters about firearms safety and how to shoot and handle the smallbore firearms. Most ranges will have equipment and gear for you to shoot, so you can explore shooting without purchasing the equipment. The range will then help you decide what firearm and gear work best for you.

How do you find a range???

National Shooting Sports Foundation (NSSF)

The NSSF has a website designed to help you locate a local range. Visit the website wheretoshoot.org or download their "Where to Shoot" app for your phone. Once you land on the first page, click the button "Find a place to shoot." This will take you to a page where you can narrow your search by state, zip

code, and the distance you want to travel. You can also select other criteria that will help you narrow your search and find the range that is best for you.

CHAPTER 3

SHOTGUN SHOOTING

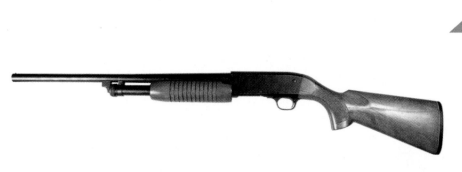

TRAP

G SPORTS

SKEET

SPORTING CLAYS

5 STAND

Photo credit: Scholastic Shooting Sports Foundation (SSSF)

Photo credit: USA Shooting Sports

Photo credit: Scholastic Shooting Sports Foundation (SSSF)

Shotguns

Shotguns are another type of firearm that shooters can shoot to enter into the shooting sports. There are several, fun and fast-paced sports you can enjoy using shotguns. In this chapter you will learn about the types of shotguns, how they are different from other firearms and activities you can participate in using shotguns.

Shotgun Safety: It's extremely important when shooting a shotgun to wear protective glasses and use some type of hearing protection. Always protect your eyes and your ears!

What is a shotgun?

A shoulder mounted, smooth bore firearm that propels either multiple small projectiles or a single projectile from a shell.

Smooth bore vs rifled bore:

Rifles have a rifled bore because of the grooves inside the barrel or bore that help to spin the projectile as it leaves the barrel to increase accuracy. Shotguns do not commonly shoot single projectiles so they do not need any grooves in the barrel. This makes the shotgun's barrel a smooth bore.

Shotguns get their name from what is typically shot out of the shotgun. Instead of a single projectile like a rifle or pistol, most shotguns shoot many small projectiles at the same time. This collection of small projectiles is called shot. Because shotguns shoot several small projectiles, the projectiles spread out as they leave the barrel making it easier to hit moving targets.

This makes shotguns very useful for hunting game that moves quickly or competitions that involve fast moving targets.

Common uses for Shotguns:

- Bird hunting
- Small game hunting
- Waterfowl hunting
- Turkey hunting
- Competition and recreational shooting

Other uses of shotguns:

- Deer hunting with deer slugs
- Self-protection

Types of Shotguns

Hinge Action Shotguns

This type of shotgun hinges in the middle of the gun and is opened up to show the chamber where the shot shell is loaded. There are three basic types of hinge action shotguns.

1. Single shot

This type only holds and shoots one shell at a time. The single shot is usually cocked by pulling back the hammer.

Advantages: Simple operation; easy for beginners to load, cock, and shoot; inexpensive
Disadvantages: Only shoots one shell, cannot shoot multiple shots quickly

2. Over and Under

This type of shotgun has two barrels stacked on top of one another. This allows two shells to be loaded and shot. This type of shotgun is cocked when the action is opened and closed. The gun is shot by pulling the trigger. Some models have one trigger that shoots both barrels, while some models have a trigger for each barrel.

Advantages: Easy to load and shoot, can shoot two shots very rapidly, can have two different chokes, commonly used in competitions
Disadvantages: Limited to only two shots, can be expensive

3. Side by Side

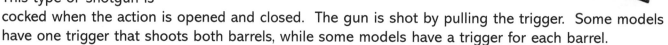

This type of shotgun is like the over and under but has two barrels that are beside each other instead of stacked. Like the over and under, it allows two shells to be loaded and shot. This type of shotgun is cocked when the action is opened and closed. However, some side by sides use a hammer to cock the gun. The gun is shot by pulling the trigger. Some models have one trigger that shoots both barrels, while some models have a trigger for each barrel.

Advantages: Easy to load and shoot, can shoot two shots very rapidly, can have two different chokes
Disadvantages: Limited to only two shots, can be expensive

Bolt action

The bolt action shotgun is loaded and cocked by lifting up the bolt handle and pulling it back to the rear and then pushing it forward to allow a shell to be moved into the chamber. Once the shell is fired, the bolt action must be repeated to load another shell. Many bolt action shotguns have a clip magazine that holds several shells.

Advantages: Easy to load and shoot, can be reloaded fairly quickly
Disadvantages: Only shoots one shell at a time before moving the action

....

Pump action

The pump action shotgun holds multiple shells in a tube magazine. The gun is loaded by sliding the foregrip back and then forward to load a new shell into the receiver. The sliding action also cocks the gun and the gun is ready to shoot. After the gun is fired, the foregrip must be slid again to remove the fired shell and load a new shell.

Advantages: Holds multiple shells, can shoot multiple shots quickly
Disadvantages: Requires coordination and multiple actions to load and shoot the gun

....

Semi-automatic

The semi-automatic action shotgun stores multiple shells in a tube magazine just like the pump shotgun. A semi-auto is loaded by pulling back the slide action of the shotgun to load a shell into the chamber. Once the gun is loaded, the gun is shot by pulling the trigger, and the fired shell is automatically removed and the next shell is automatically loaded into the chamber. This allows the gun to be shot just by pulling the trigger with no other cocking action being required.

Advantages: Holds multiple shells, can shoot multiple shots very quickly, less recoil
Disadvantages: More expensive than pump shotguns

Parts of a Shotgun

Parts of an over and under shotgun

STOCK · SAFETY · BARREL RELEASE · FOREGRIP · VENTILATED RIB · SIGHTING BEAD · BARREL · MUZZLE · TRIGGER · TRIGGER GUARD · BUTT PLATE

Parts of a pump shotgun

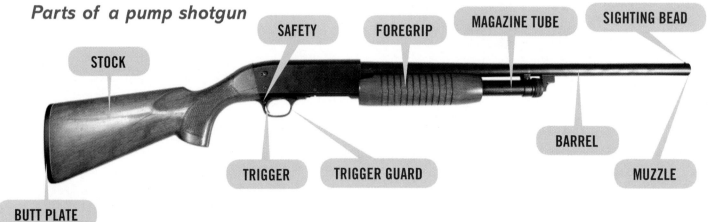

SAFETY · FOREGRIP · MAGAZINE TUBE · SIGHTING BEAD · STOCK · TRIGGER · TRIGGER GUARD · BARREL · MUZZLE · BUTT PLATE

Parts of a semi-automatic shotgun

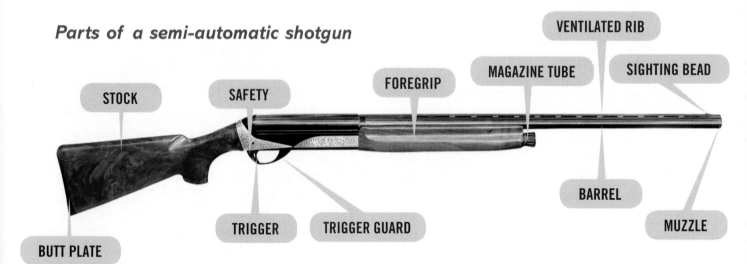

VENTILATED RIB · MAGAZINE TUBE · SIGHTING BEAD · FOREGRIP · STOCK · SAFETY · TRIGGER · TRIGGER GUARD · BARREL · MUZZLE · BUTT PLATE

What ammunition do shotguns shoot?

If you remember from the smallbore chapter, rifles shoot cartridges. Shotguns do not shoot cartridges, they shoot shotshells. So what makes up a shotshell?

Parts of a Shotshell

Unprimed hull – this is the part of the shell that holds all of the other parts. The hull is usually made of plastic and has a base made of brass. The hull is considered "unprimed" if it does not have a primer in the brass base.

Primer – this part is placed in the center of the brass base of the hull. When the firing pin hits the primer the primer makes a tiny explosion that catches the powder on fire.

Powder – the powder burns very quickly and creates a lot of gases as it burns. The gas expands and tries to leave the barrel. As the gas leaves the barrel, the gas pushes the wad that is next to it.

Wad – the wad is a plastic part that fits into the hull and between the powder and the shot. The wad forms a cup that holds the shot together inside the hull.

Shot – the shot are the small round projectiles the shotgun will shoot. The shot comes in different sizes. This will be discussed later in the chapter.

The top of the hull is crimped, which means it is pushed down to form a tightly sealed top to keep the shot from falling out of the hull.

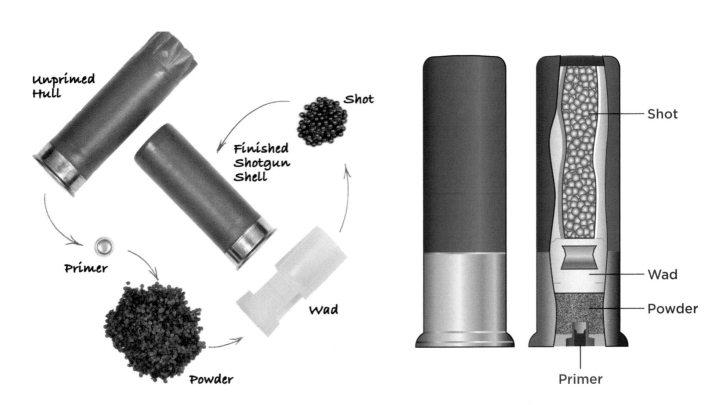

Sizes of Shotshells

It is very important that the correct gauge shotshell is used in the correct gauge shotgun. To help shooters to identify the correct gauge, each shotshell has the gauge size stamped into the  brass on the bottom of the shell. This is the best way to identify the gauge of the shotshell because some gauges are very similar in size.

Warning!: Some smaller gauge shells can actually fit into the chamber of a larger gauge shotgun and slide down out of sight. If a shell of the correct gauge is then loaded into the chamber and is shot, the first shell can block the barrel and cause the barrel to explode.

This can result in severe injury to the shooter, or even death. ALWAYS BE SURE YOU LOAD THE CORRECT GAUGE SHELL INTO A SHOTGUN AND ALWAYS SHOOT WITH ADULT SUPERVISION!

What is a Gauge?

If you remember, rifle sizes were measured in caliber. Shotguns are measured by gauges. So what is a gauge? Like caliber, gauge has to do with the diameter of the barrel, or bore as it is called in a shotgun. Here is how it works:

The bore of the shotgun is measured to find the diameter. For example, a 12 gauge bore has a diameter of 0.729 inches.

Lead balls that are the same diameter of the barrel, 0.729 inches, are made it find out the gauge. The number of those lead balls that make a pound is the gauge of that shotgun.

In the case of a 12 gauge, it takes 12 lead balls that are 0.729 inches in diameter to make one pound. So, it is called a 12 gauge.

A 20 gauge shotgun bore is 0.615 inches in diameter. How may lead balls that size make up one pound? You guessed it, 20. That was easy wasn't it?

Exception to the Rule:
The only exception to the gauges of a shotgun is the .410. The .410 is actually like a rifle cartridge. It is the actual diameter of the bore or the caliber. So, .410 is the actual diameter of the bore, 0.410 inches. Because of this, .410 is a caliber, not a gauge.

Other Size Factors for Shotgun Shells

Length

When you look for shotgun shells to buy, you may see they come in different lengths. For example, you can buy 12 gauge shells that are 2 ¾ inches, 3 inches, or even 3 ½ inches long.

Which is best? First, you should know what length of shells your shotgun can shoot. Not all shotguns can shoot all lengths of shells. The length of shells the shotgun can shoot is stamped on the side of the barrel.

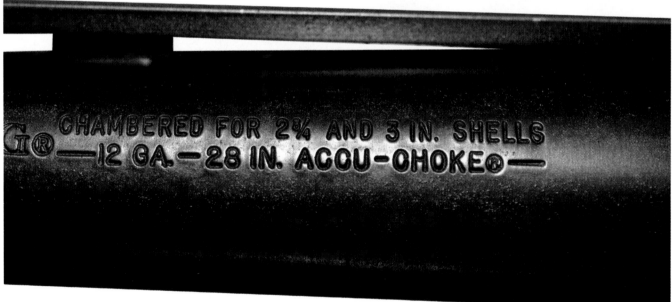

All shotguns can shoot the standard length shell which is 2 ¾ inches long. Longer shells are typically used for hunting situations where the shooter needs the gun to shoot longer distances or more shot. All shotgun shooting sports use 2 ¾ inch shells.

Shot Size and Material

Shot is the most common projectile shot from a shotgun. These small projectiles come in many different sizes and can be made from different materials. The most common material is lead. However, there are laws for waterfowl hunting that require hunters to use shot made from non-toxic materials such as steel, tungsten or other metals instead of lead.

Shot size is given by numbers. Shot sizes range from #12 to OO buckshot. The funny thing about shot sizes is that the higher the number is, the smaller the size of the shot. For example, #6 shot is smaller than #4 shot. When you look for shotshells to shoot in your shotgun, you should pick the size shot and material that is best for the targets you will be shooting.

If you are shooting skeet, use #9 lead shot. For trap and sporting clays, shooters shoot #8 ½ to #7 ½ lead shot. Upland bird hunters shoot #7 ½, while turkey hunters may shoot up to #4 lead shot. Waterfowl hunters can use #6 to #4 steel or other non-toxic shot for ducks and up to BBB or F steel or other non-toxic shot for larger geese.

Shot Size Chart

Lead shot sizes:	12	9	8$^{1/2}$	8	7$^{1/2}$	6	5	4	2	BB
Pellet diameter (inches)	.05	.080	.085	.095	.080	.110	.120	.130	.150	.180
(mm)	1.27	2.30	2.16	2.29	2.41	2.79	3.05	3.30	3.81	4.57

Buckshot sizes:	No. 4	No. 3	No. 2	No. 1	No. 0	No. 00	No. 000
Pellet diameter (inches)	.24	.25	.27	.30	.32	.33	.36
(mm)	6.10	6.35	6.86	7.62	8.13	8.38	9.14

Steel shot sizes:	6	5	4	3	2	1	Air Rifle	BB	BBB	T	F
Pellet diameter (inches)	.11	.12	.13	.14	.15	.16	.177	.18	.19	.20	.22
(mm)	2.79	3.05	3.30	3.56	3.81	4.06	4.49	4.57	4.83	5.08	5.59

Note: the size of shot, whether lead or steel, is based on American Standard shot sizes.
Thus, a steel No. 4 pellet and a lead No. 4 pellet are both .13 inches (3.3mm) in diameter.

Shooting Your Shotgun

Once you have decided the type of shotgun is best for you and the shotshells that are best for what you are shooting, you may need to make one more decision. That decision is what choke to use in your shotgun.

Depending on the shotgun, either the barrel is made with a specific choke or the barrel has removable choke tubes that can be changed for different shooting situations. These removable chokes screw into the end of the barrel. A special tool called a choke tube wrench is used to insert and remove the choke tubes.

Different types of chokes control the pattern of the shot. So what is the pattern of shot? The pattern of shot is the group of shot or pellets that hit a target at a certain distance.

Choke:

the tapered or narrowed section at the end of a shotgun barrel's muzzle. The choke is designed to control the pattern of the shot fired from the gun to control the spread of the shot.

Tight Pattern

Small pattern with many pellets in a small circle.

Open Pattern

Larger pattern or circle with with less pellets in the circle.

Here is another way of thinking about chokes.

A choke controls how narrow the end of the muzzle will be, much like a garden hose nozzle can control how narrow the opening is where the water leaves the garden hose and the pattern of the water stream.

If you want the water stream to be narrow and go the farthest distance, you want the opening of the nozzle to be very narrow. This is what a full or extra-full choke does.

If you want the water stream to be really wide but not go so far, you want the nozzle opening to be wider. This is what an improved cylinder choke does.

There are several different types of chokes that can be used for different shooting situations.

Types of Chokes

The most common chokes are full, modified and improved cylinder. Here is some information about each of these chokes.

Full choke
This is the most narrow of the chokes and is used for longer distance shooting.

Modified choke
This is a more open choke and not as narrow. This choke is probably the best all-around choke for shooting.

Improved Cylinder choke
This choke is wider than the other two and is used to shoot targets at a closer range.

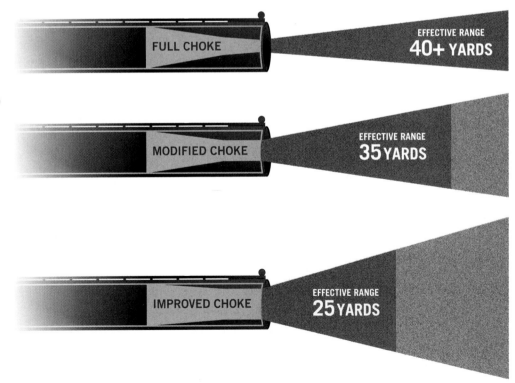

FULL CHOKE — EFFECTIVE RANGE **40+ YARDS**

MODIFIED CHOKE — EFFECTIVE RANGE **35 YARDS**

IMPROVED CHOKE — EFFECTIVE RANGE **25 YARDS**

Facts About the Different Types of Chokes

Choke Type	Effective Distance Range (yards)	Choke restriction (Diameter difference in inches between the bore and choke)	Percent of shot or pellets hitting the target at 40 yards
Cylinder	Less than 20	0	40
Skeet	22.5	0.005	45
Improved cylinder	25	0.10	50
Modified	32.5	0.020	60
Improved modified	35	0.025	65
Full	40 or more	0.035	70
Extra-full	40 or more	0.040	70+

Sighting a Shotgun

Shotguns are unique because they are meant to be pointed and not aimed. Since the shotgun usually shoots several projectiles or shot, you just need to point the gun in the direction you are shooting to hit your target. Other guns that shoot a single projectile must be aimed so the single projectile hits exactly where you are shooting.

Shotguns can have many different types of sights. The most common sights on a shotgun are bead sights. Some shotguns have a single bead at the end of the barrel, while some have two or double beads. Double bead sights have one bead at the end of the barrel and another about half way down the barrel. These sights are the sights commonly used in shotgun shooting sports.

To sight a single bead shotgun, the shooter looks down the barrel and covers the target with the bead or places it slightly in front of the target if it is moving. Sighting a double bead shotgun is similar. However, the shooter looks down the barrel and lines up BOTH beads with the target. Lining up both beads forces shooters to keep their cheek on the stock while shooting and not pull their head up when they pull the trigger. Keeping your head down and making sure both beads are lined up with the target will make you a more accurate shooter.

Other shotgun sights

There are other sights used on some shotguns but these are mainly used to shoot targets that are standing still. Many shotguns used to shoot turkey or deer use these types of sights. These other types of sights include iron sights or blade sights, holographic sights, red-dot sights and telescopic sights.

Beaded Sights

Holographic Sights

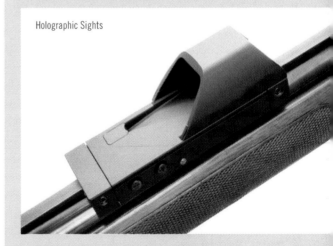

Practicing your Shooting Skills

The shotgun shooting sports, as well as many different hunting situations, requires shooters to be able to shoot moving or flying targets. For this reason, it is important to practice these skills to become the best shooter you can be. The most common target used for shotguns is the clay pigeon or target.

Back in the 1800s, the only way to practice was to release live birds from traps positioned in front of the shooter. Because of the need for numerous live birds, this practice was replaced with shooting glass balls that mimicked the shooting of actual birds. Eventually, these glass balls were replaced with circular discs made from clay.

Those discs or clay targets are still used today and have been improved so they can be thrown and move more like a bird's actual flight. The modern clay target is an upside down saucer shape and is made from a mixture of pitch (resin) and limestone. Many of these targets are now biodegradable, which means they will break down naturally if left out in the environment. These targets are tough enough to be thrown at high speeds, but fragile enough to break if they are hit by just a few pellets.

Modern clay targets come in many sizes and colors; however, the most common colors are orange and black. Targets are made to specific size and weights, depending on the sport.

Here are some facts about the types of clay targets:

Standard
- This is the target most people are familiar with and commonly see or shoot.
- It is designed to fly in the air for long distances.
- It is a versatile target and can be used in any type of shooting.
- The size is 108-110 mm in diameter by 25-29 mm high and each target weighs 100-105 grams.

Rabbit
- This target is similar in size to the standard target but not designed to fly.
- These targets are designed to be rolled across the ground to move like a running rabbit.
- The size is 108-110 mm in diameter.

Midi
- This is similar to the standard target but only 90 mm in diameter.
- It is designed to fly faster than the standard target.

Mini
- This is the smallest of the clay targets.
- It is only 60 mm in diameter and 20 mm in height.
- It is designed to fly very fast.

Target Throwers

All of the targets just listed above, except for the rabbit, are meant to be thrown and fly through the air. To make the targets fly through the air, you need something to throw them. Target throwers can range from very simple and inexpensive to very complex and expensive.

Warning!: No matter what type of thrower you use to practice your shooting, you must have the thrower pointed down range into an open area away from buildings, traffic or people. You must always be sure of your target and what is beyond it. You should only practice your shooting skills with adult supervision!

Hand Throwers

A hand thrower is a plastic tool made to manually throw the clay target into the air.

Advantages: Very simple and affordable way to get started shooting clay targets.

Disadvantages: Limited speed and distance the clay target travels.
Requires one person to throw the target while another is shooting.

Mechanical Throwers

This type of thrower does not require manpower to throw the clay target. It throws the target using a mechanical device. There are two basic types of mechanical throwers.

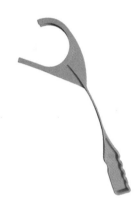

Spring-type Thrower

This type of thrower uses a very powerful spring to throw the clay targets.

Advantages: Least expensive of the mechanical throwers.
Throws targets faster than hand thrower.
Targets released by simple process of pulling a string.

Disadvantages: The spring mechanism must be pulled back or cocked by hand and loaded by hand.
The strong spring mechanism can cause injury if not used properly.

Electronic Thrower

This type of thrower is electronically powered and released and can hold several clay targets.

Advantages: Does not require any manpower to cock.
Holds several targets, so the thrower does not have to be loaded often.
Can be activated or triggered to throw the targets with a remote.
Throws clay targets at a fast speed.

Disadvantages: Most expensive type of thrower.
Requires a battery or electricity to operate.

Shotgun Shooting Sports

Trapshooting

The sport of trapshooting, or trap as it is sometimes called, is an event where clay targets are thrown into the air at different directions. The goal is to hit the target every time to get the highest score.

This activity has its roots in the 1700s when men took live birds and placed them under hats or boxes. The birds were released and the men would shoot at the birds like they were in a hunting situation. By the 1800s laws were passed that banned the use of live birds, so man-made birds were created and the sport of trapshooting began.

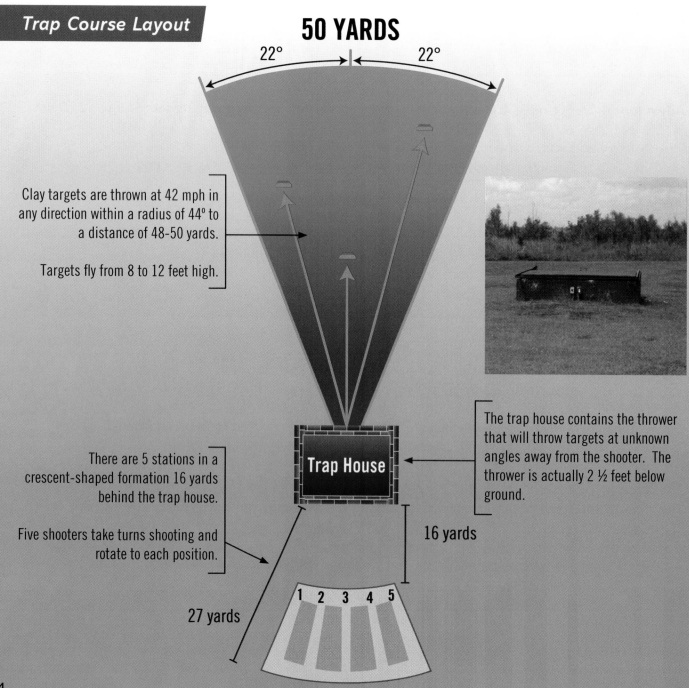

Trap Course Layout

50 YARDS

22°   22°

Clay targets are thrown at 42 mph in any direction within a radius of 44° to a distance of 48-50 yards.

Targets fly from 8 to 12 feet high.

The trap house contains the thrower that will throw targets at unknown angles away from the shooter. The thrower is actually 2 ½ feet below ground.

Trap House

There are 5 stations in a crescent-shaped formation 16 yards behind the trap house.

Five shooters take turns shooting and rotate to each position.

16 yards

1 2 3 4 5

27 yards

How the sport of trap works:

1. Five shooters line up in the 5 different positions on the trap field.
2. The shooter in the #1 position will shoot first and shoot a single shot at a single target.
3. Shooting is then done in a rotation so the shooter in position #2 shoots next, then the next position shoots, and so on.
4. Each shooter will fire 5 shots from their first position, then they will rotate one position to the right. 1 to 2, 2 to 3, 3 to 4, 4 to 5, and 5 to 1.
5. Shooters will then shoot 5 shots in rotation from the new position and then rotate again.
6. Shooters will rotate until they have fired 5 shots at each of the 5 positions for a total of 25 shots.
7. The score depends on the number of targets "hit." If a target is hit or shatters it is considered "dead." The final score is the number of dead targets out of 25. So if you hit 20 targets, the score would be 20/25.

Trap Lingo

Pull – word used to signal that you are ready to shoot, and for a target to be released.

Dead target – any target that has a visible piece broken from the target or if the target is totally shattered by the shot.

Lost target – any target fired upon by the shooter that has no visible broken pieces.

No target – any target thrown where no score is recorded.

Singles – trap event where single targets are shot at a distance of 16 yards.

Doubles – trap event where two targets are thrown at the same time and both must be shot at a distance of 16 yards.

Handicap – event where shooters shoot at single targets from a distance of 18 to 27 yards depending on how good a shooter they are.

Trapshooting Equipment

Shooting trap only requires some basic equipment and gear:

Shotgun

- Single shot, over and under, pump or semi-automatic will work
- 20 gauge or larger, with 12 gauge being the most popular
- .410 can be used but takes more skill
- Beginning shooters should use modified chokes, while experienced shooters may use full chokes

Shotshells – Use #8 or #9 shot

Eye protection – A good pair of quality shooting glasses

Ear protection – Shotguns are loud and quality shooting ear muffs or earplugs work well

Shooting vest or shell holders
- Shooters need a place to hold their live and spent shotshells as they shoot
- Shooters can use a vest or a shell pouch to hold their shotshells

Trapshooting Manners

When you shoot trap, there are obviously rules and procedures that must be followed. However, there are some important "manners" or etiquette you should follow as you shoot at the trap range.

- Do not raise your gun until the shooter ahead of you fires.
- Remain in your shooting position until the 5th shooter has fired, then move to the next position.
- Never load your gun before changing positions.
- Load only a single shell at a time and only close the action of the gun when it is your turn to shoot.
- There should be no unnecessary talking when standing at the firing line.
- When it is your time to shoot, call in a loud, clear voice so the rangemaster knows you are ready.
- Observe all gun safety rules. Always be aware of where the muzzle of your gun is pointing. When on the firing line, the gun should always be pointed at the trap house or toward the ground.

A Few Tips or Tricks to Trapshooting

Obviously, there is a lot that goes into becoming a very good trapshooter. It takes practice and dedication to score consistently high scores in trap. However, there are a few things you can do to score better and help you keep track of your score.

Shooting Tips:

- The quicker the shot is fired, the better chance of hitting the target because the target will be closer.
- Keep moving your gun after you take the shot. This is called "**follow through**" and is very important to accurate shooting.
- Always lead (point slightly ahead) the target if it is moving at an angle from you. This gives the shot time to reach the target.

Scoring Tip:

Some places where you shoot trap will have scorers who keep track of the score. If you don't have a scorer, an easy way to keep track of your score, or your hits and misses, is to place your shells in a certain pocket for hits and a different pocket for misses. At the end, you can count the shells in the "hit" pocket to know how many you hit or scored.

Scoring trap on the range.

Skeet

Skeet is a sport where clay targets are thrown from two fixed positions at different heights. Shooters use shotguns to shoot from 8 different positions on the skeet course. The sport of skeet was actually created in Massachusetts in 1920 by a group of bird hunters. These hunters wanted a more realistic way of imitating every shot they may take while bird hunting.

Fun Fact

The word "skeet" is actually an old Scandinavian form of the word "shoot."

They started by "shooting around the clock," meaning the course was like a clock face with a 50 yard diameter. The thrower was placed at the 12 o'clock position, and threw targets toward the 6 o'clock position. Each shooter would shoot from every position. This was fine until the neighbor's chickens were being affected by the shot falling from the sky. As you see in the diagram of this first course below, shots were going in every direction and safety was difficult to control unless the course was located in a large open area.

Original Skeet Course Layout

Because of these safety concerns, the skeet course was changed to half of a clock face and the throwers placed at 12 and 6 o'clock. This allowed shooters to all shoot in one direction and keep the shots going down range and not in all different directions.

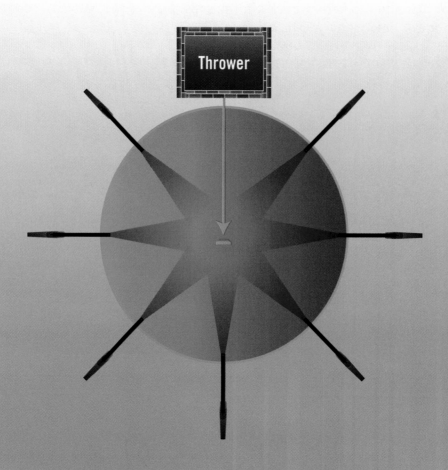

Modern Skeet Course Layout

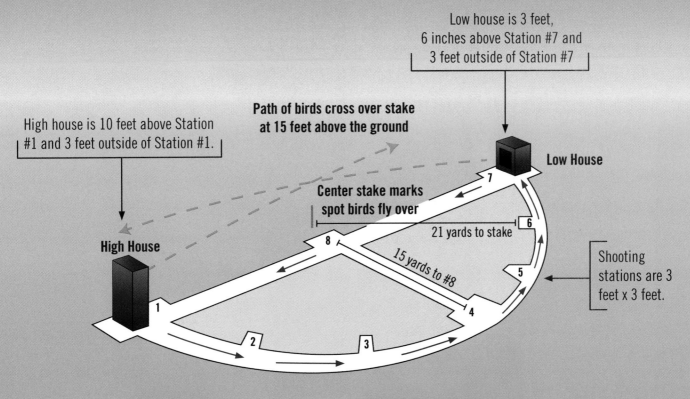

Low house is 3 feet, 6 inches above Station #7 and 3 feet outside of Station #7.

Path of birds cross over stake at 15 feet above the ground

High house is 10 feet above Station #1 and 3 feet outside of Station #1.

Center stake marks spot birds fly over

Low House

High House

21 yards to stake

15 yards to #8

Shooting stations are 3 feet x 3 feet.

How the Sport of Skeet works

High house single – *single target thrown from the high house thrower when the shooter calls "Pull."*

High House

Stations 1 and 2

1. First shooter starts at Station #1 and will shoot a high house single shot.
2. Next, the shooter will shoot a low house single shot. The final shot is a double, meaning two shells are loaded and the shooter will have to shoot two targets. One target from the high house and one target from the low house will be thrown at the same time. (The high house shot is taken first.)
3. The remaining four shooters will each repeat this sequence.
4. Station 2 is shot with the same sequence of shots as Station 1.
5. **Each shooter shoots a total of 4 shots at each station.**

Stations 3, 4, and 5

1. The first shooter loads two shells and will shoot a high house single first, then a low house single.
2. The remaining shooters repeat this sequence at Station 3.
3. All shooters will repeat the same shot sequence of station 3 for stations 4 and 5.
4. **Each shooter shoots a total of 2 shots at each station.**

Station 8

1. The first shooter loads two shells and shoots a high house single, followed by a low house single.
2. If the shooter has not missed any targets, then the 25th shot is another low house single.
3. The target must be hit before it reaches the crossing point or it is counted as a miss.

Low house single –
single target thrown from the low house thrower when the shooter calls "Pull."

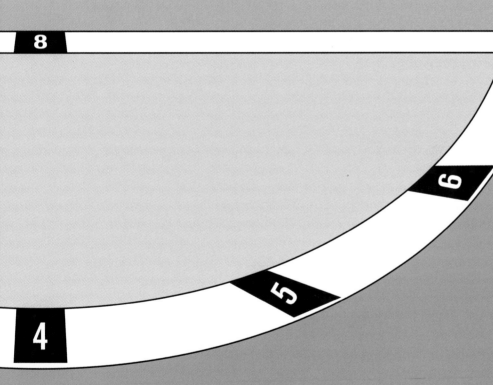

Low House

Stations 6 and 7

1. These stations are similar to stations 1 and 2 with one major difference.
2. First shooter starts at Station 6 and will shoot a high house single shot and then a low house single shot.
3. The shooter will then reload and get ready for a double.
4. One target from the high house and one target from the low house will be thrown at the same time, **BUT for this station, the low house shot is taken first**.
5. The remaining four shooters will each repeat this sequence for station 6.
6. Station 7 is shot with the same sequence of shots as Station 6.
7. **Each shooter shoots a total of 4 shots at each station.**

Double – One target from the high house and one target from the low house will be thrown at the same time. (The high house shot is taken first.)

Key to Shooting Skeet

The key to shooting skeet successfully is the lead. Skeet is a sport of mathematics, geometry, and physics all wrapped into one game. It is all about speed, time, and distance. The targets in skeet travel very fast at some difficult angles. This means it can take beginner shooters some time to master the sport.

According to a study done by the National Skeet Shooting Association (NSSA), a beginner shooter can expect to break 11 out of 25 targets on their first try. Beginners can expect to gradually improve to scoring high teens or low twenties with practice. A perfect score of 25 is very possible with practice and patience.

The main thing that beginning shooters must master is the lead. The lead is how far out in front of the target you point the barrel as you shoot. This distance you lead the target allows for the time to pull the trigger, the shell to fire, and the shot to reach the target's path.

Quick Tips:

- The key is to pull the trigger quickly when you think you have the correct distance of lead, and KEEP the end of your barrel moving with the target after you pull the trigger (follow through). If you wait too long or do not follow through, you will miss the target.
- When moving your gun, make sure it is on the same horizontal plane as the target. If you are pointing above or below the target, you will certainly miss. Shooting over the target is the most common mistake.
- Make sure when shooting that the target is just ON or just ABOVE the front bead of your shotgun. If you are not consistent with this, you will usually shoot over the target.

Suggested Leads for the Different Shots at each Station

House Thrower	Station 1	Station 2	Station 3	Station 4	Station 5	Station 6	Station 7	Station 8
High	None	1-2$^{1/2}$ feet	4-4$^{1/2}$ feet	4-4$^{1/2}$ feet	4-4$^{1/2}$ feet	2-2$^{1/2}$ feet	10-12 feet	None
Low	10-12 feet	2-2$^{1/2}$ feet	4-4$^{1/2}$ feet	4-4$^{1/2}$ feet	4-4$^{1/2}$ feet	1-2$^{1/2}$ feet	None	None

Skeet Shooting Equipment

If you want to shoot skeet, you will need similar equipment and gear as trapshooting with a few differences:

Shotgun

- Over and under, pump or semi-automatic that will hold two shells will work
- 12, 20, 28 gauges, and .410 bore are used in the four classes of skeet
- Skeet choke or improved cylinder choke are most common
- The key is to have the gun fit the shooter well

Shotshells – Use #7 1/2 or #9 shotshells loaded with 1 ounce of shot

Eye protection – A good pair of quality shooting glasses

Ear protection – Shotguns are loud and quality shooting ear muffs or earplugs work well

Shooting vest or shell holders

- Shooters need a place to hold their live and spent shotshells as they shoot
- Shooters can use a vest or a shell pouch to hold their shotshells

Manners on the Skeet Range

Like shooting trap, there are rules and procedures that must be followed when shooting skeet. Here are some important "manners" or etiquette you should follow as you shoot at the skeet range.

- When not shooting, always keep the action of the gun open. This way there is no question the gun is loaded.
- Never load your gun until you are on a station and it is your turn to shoot. It is okay to load two shells in skeet because you take 2 shots.
- There should be no unnecessary talking when standing at the stations.
- When it is your time to shoot, call in a loud, clear voice so the rangemaster knows you are ready.
- Observe all gun safety rules. Always be aware of where the muzzle of your gun is pointing. When on the firing line, your gun should always be pointed at or toward the ground.

Sporting Clays

Sporting clays is the shotgun sport that is the closest to hunting in the field. A sporting clays course is laid out over natural terrain and surroundings and typically includes 10-15 shooting stations. The sporting clays course is usually no smaller than 30 acres to ensure the safety of all of the shooters.

Because a sporting clays course is so large and spread out, shooters have to travel to each station, much like golfers have to travel to each hole on a golf course. This is why many people call sporting clays "golf with a shotgun."

What makes sporting clays different than trap and skeet?

*   Sporting clay targets are thrown at different angles, distances, speeds, and elevations.
*   The size of sporting clay targets are different from station to station.
*   Targets are thrown to simulate many different hunting situations, such as ducks, pheasants, quail, doves, and rabbits.
*   Targets may be shot over water, through trees, from under foot, straight over your head, and from left to right and from right to left.
*   Every sporting clays course is different.

How Sporting Clays is played

Basics of the Sport:

Shooters will shoot a course with 10-15 stations.
Each station may throw 5 to 10 targets.
Targets can be singles or pairs.
Ways the pairs can be thrown:
*   True pair – targets thrown at the same time
*   Following pair – targets thrown one after another
*   Report pair – the second target is thrown on the "report" of the shooter's gun (sound of the shot)

Shooting the Course:

1. A "squad" which is a group of 2-6 shooters begins at an assigned station.
2. The course referee will show the squad how all of the targets for that station are thrown for shooters to develop a game plan of how they will shoot the station.
3. After seeing the practice targets, each shooter in the squad will take turns shooting all of the targets for that station.
4. When the squad is finished shooting the station, squad members open the actions of their guns and leave the station and travel to the next station.
5. If shooters at the next station are not finished, the squad must wait behind the station until that squad is finished and moves to the next station.

Scoring Sporting Clays

Scores are based on how many "dead" targets are shot (any break of the clay target). Score is usually out of 100 shots.

Safety Reminder: When shooting sporting clays, all rules of firearm safety must be followed. Like all shotgun shooting sports, it is very important to handle your gun in a safe manner.

Sporting Clays Equipment

If you want to shoot sporting clays, you will need similar equipment and gear as trapshooting and skeet shooting:

Shotgun

- Over and under, pump or semi-automatic that will hold two shells will work
- 12 and 20 gauges are most common but 28 gauges and .410 bore can be used
- Skeet choke or improved cylinder choke

Shotshells – Use #7 1/2 or #9 shotshells

Eye protection – A good pair of quality shooting glasses

Ear protection – Shotguns are loud and quality shooting ear muffs or earplugs work well

Shooting vest or shell holders

- Shooters need a place to hold their live and spent shotshells as they shoot
- Shooters can use a vest or a shell pouch to hold their shells

National Sporting Clays Association (NSCA) rule book

The NSCA rule book can be found and downloaded at:
http://www.nssa-nsca.org/wp-content/uploads/2015/02/2015-NSCA-Rule-Book-2-11-151.pdf

Five Stand

The sport of five stand is very similar to sporting clays because the targets are thrown in a variety of ways. The main difference is that there are five stationary stands that shooters will shoot from. Shooters do not have to travel distances to shoot the different types of shots that are seen in sporting clays.

Five Stand Course

- Like trap, the five stand course has 5 stations where 1 to 5 shooters shoot.
- Each shooter will shoot 5 shots from each station and then rotate to the right.
- The course is set up with 5 to 20 throwers placed anywhere around the shooters. This allows targets to come from every direction, giving the shooter a realistic hunting experience.
- Targets can fly straight up, fly toward you, come from behind you, roll on the ground, or make giant arcs.

There are no set standards where targets have to come from, nor is there a set way the trap throwers must be set. Any set up can be done with five stand.

How the Sport of Five Stand is Played

1. Shooters take their position in one of the five positions.
2. The shooter to the farthest left position shoots first.

3. First shot is a single bird and you get two shots, if needed.
4. The next stand station (#2) will probably be a different type of shot. (It is good to pay attention to where the target is flying because you will be shooting that position next, if you are shooter #1.)
5. After everyone has shot a single at their station, the next shot will be a pair on report.
6. The shooter yells "pull" and the first target is thrown, and the second target is thrown at the sound of the first shot.
7. All shooters will shoot a pair on report at their station, but the pairs are usually different.
8. The last shot will be a true double, so both targets are thrown when the shooter yells "pull." (You must be quick to get shots at both targets.) NOTE: It is allowed to use both shots on the first target if the shooter so chooses.
9. All shooters shoot the true double for their station, which again will probably be different.
10. After this shot the group rotates to the right and repeats the whole shooting sequence.
11. The group rotates to each station until all shooters have shot at all five stations.
12. The score is the number of targets shot out of 25 shots.

Five Stand Gear

The gear for five stand is the same as for sporting clays.

Photo credit: Scholastic Shooting Sports Foundation (SSSF)

CHAPTER 4

SHOOTING SPORTS

EAR AND EYE PROTECTION MANDATORY

ACTIONS OPEN AT ALL TIMES

SAFETY

HANDLING FIREARMS SAFELY	SAFETY GEAR	RANGE SAFETY

Shooting Sports Safety

As you have read, shooting sports are some of the safest sporting activities. The reason they are safe is because responsible shooters follow strict safety rules. When you participate in any shooting sport, you must always handle your firearm safely, use the correct safety gear, and always follow the basic rules of firearms safety and all range safety rules when shooting on a range.

It is very important that you read this chapter and understand shooting sports and firearms safety, so you can be one of those participants who enjoys some of the safest activities there are to offer. If you put these important safety guidelines into practice and always shoot with adult supervision, your shooting sports experiences will always be safe and enjoyable.

Handling Firearms Safely

Below are 10 Rules of Safe Gun Handling that the National Shooting Sports Foundation (NSSF) shares with shooters to promote gun safety. If you follow these 10 rules you should always be safe on the range or in the field. Thanks to the NSSF for providing these important safety rules.

1. Always Keep The Muzzle Pointed In A Safe Direction

This is the most basic safety rule. If everyone handled a firearm so carefully that the muzzle never pointed at something they didn't intend to shoot, there would be virtually no firearms accidents. It's as simple as that, and it's up to you.

Never point your gun at anything you do not intend to shoot. This is particularly important when loading or unloading a firearm. In the event a gun would go off accidentally, no injury can occur as long as the muzzle is pointing in a safe direction.

A safe direction means a direction in which a bullet cannot possibly hit anyone, including possible ricochets and the fact that bullets can go through walls and ceilings. The safe direction may be "up" on some occasions or "down" on others, but never at anyone. Even when "dry firing" with an unloaded gun, you should never point the gun at an unsafe target.

Make it a habit to know exactly where the muzzle of your gun is pointing at all times, and be sure that you are in control of the direction in which the muzzle is pointing, even if you fall or stumble. This is your responsibility, and only you can control it.

2. Firearms Should Be Unloaded When Not Actually In Use

Firearms should be loaded only when you are in the field or on the target range or shooting area, ready to shoot. When not being used, firearms and ammunition should be stored in a safe place, separate from each other. Children and youth should not be allowed access to firearms or ammunition. This should only be done by an adult.

Unload your gun as soon as you are finished. A loaded gun has no place in or near a car, truck, or building. Unload your gun immediately when you have finished shooting, well before you take it to a car, camp, or home.

Whenever you handle a firearm or hand it to someone, always open the action immediately, and look in the chamber,

receiver, and magazine to be certain they do not contain any ammunition. Always keep actions open when not in use. Never assume a gun is unloaded, check for yourself! This is considered a mark of an experienced gun handler!

Never cross a fence, climb a tree, or perform any awkward action with a loaded gun. While in the field, there will be times when common sense and the basic rules of firearms safety will require you to unload your gun to be perfectly safe. Never pull or push a loaded firearm toward yourself or another person. There is never any excuse to carry a loaded gun in a holster when not being worn or in a gun case. When in doubt, unload your gun!

3. Don't Rely On Your Gun's "Safety"

Treat every gun like it can fire at any time. The "safety" on any gun is a mechanical device which, like any such device, can fail or not work at the worst possible time. By mistake, the safety may be "off" when you think it is "on." The safety serves as an additional step to proper gun handling but cannot be a substitute for common sense. You should never handle a gun carelessly and assume that the gun won't fire just because the "safety is on."

Never touch the trigger on a firearm until you intend to shoot. Keep your fingers away from the trigger while loading or unloading. Never pull the trigger on any firearm with the safety on the "safe" position or anywhere in between "safe" and "fire." It is possible that the gun can fire at any time, or even later when you release the safety, without your ever touching the trigger again.

Never place the safety in between positions, since half-safe is unsafe. Keep the safety "on" until you are absolutely ready to fire.

No matter what the position of the safety may be, any strong hit or jar to the gun may be enough to make the firing mechanism of a gun fire. This can happen even if the trigger is not touched, such as when a gun is dropped. Never rest a loaded gun against any object. There is always the possibility that it will be hit or slide from its position and fall with a force to make it fire. The only time you can be absolutely certain that a gun cannot fire is when the action is open and it is completely empty. Again, never rely on your gun's safety. You and the safe gun handling procedures you learned are your gun's primary safeties.

4. Be Sure Of Your Target And What's Beyond It

No one can call a shot back. Once a gun fires, you have given up all control over where the shot will go or what it will hit. Don't shoot unless you know exactly what your shot is going to hit. Be sure that your bullet will not injure anyone or anything beyond your target. Firing at a movement or a noise without knowing exactly what you are shooting at means you are not thinking about the safety of others. No target is so important that you cannot take the time before you pull the trigger to be absolutely sure of your target and where your shot will stop.

Be aware that even a .22 short bullet can travel over 1 1/4 miles and a high velocity rifle cartridge, such as a 30-06, can send its bullet more than 3 miles. Shotgun pellets can travel 500 yards, and shotgun slugs have a range of over half a mile.

You should keep in mind how far a bullet will travel if it misses your intended target or ricochets in another direction.

5. Use Correct Ammunition

You and an adult must always be sure you are using only the correct ammunition for your firearm. Read and heed all warnings, including those that appear in the gun's instruction manual and on the ammunition boxes.

Using improper or incorrect ammunition can destroy a gun and cause serious injury to you and others around you. It only takes one cartridge of improper caliber or gauge to destroy your gun, and only a second to check each one as you load it. Be absolutely certain that the ammunition you are using matches the information in the gun's instruction manual and the manufacturer's markings on the firearm.

Firearms are designed, made, and proof tested to standards based upon those of factory loaded ammunition. Handloaded or reloaded ammunition that may be different from pressures created by factory loads or from recommendations explained in reputable handloading manuals can be dangerous, and can cause severe damage to guns and serious injury to the shooter. Do not use improper reloads or ammunition made of unknown parts.

Ammunition that has become very wet or has been under water should be discarded in a safe manner. Do not spray oil or solvents on ammunition or place ammunition in firearms that have been heavily oiled. Poor ignition, unsatisfactory performance, or damage to your firearm and harm to yourself or others could result from using such ammunition.

Form the habit of checking every cartridge you put into your gun. Never use damaged or poor, cheap ammunition. The money saved is not worth the risk of possible injury or a ruined gun.

NOTE: Discharging firearms in poorly ventilated areas, cleaning firearms, or handling ammunition may result in exposure to lead and other substances known to cause health hazards and other serious physical injury. Have adequate ventilation at all times and wash your hands thoroughly after shooting and handling ammunition.

6. If Your Gun Fails To Fire When The Trigger Is Pulled, Handle With Care!

Sometimes, a cartridge may not fire when the trigger is pulled. If this occurs, keep the muzzle pointed in a safe direction. Keep your face away from the breech. Then, carefully open the action, unload the firearm and dispose of the cartridge in a safe way.

Any time there is a cartridge in the chamber, your gun is loaded and ready to fire even if you've tried to shoot and it did not go off. It could go off at any time, so you must always remember Rule #1 and watch that muzzle!

7. Always Wear Eye And Ear Protection When Shooting

All shooters should wear protective shooting glasses and some form of hearing protectors while shooting. Exposure to shooting noise can damage hearing, and good eye protection is essential. Shooting glasses guard against twigs, falling shot, clay target chips, and the rare firearm malfunction. Wearing eye protection when disassembling and cleaning any gun will also help prevent the possibility of gun parts, oil, and cleaning chemicals from contacting your eyes. There is a wide variety of eye and ear protectors available. No target shooter, plinker, or hunter should ever be without them.

Most rules of shooting safety are intended to protect you and others around you, but this rule is for your protection alone. Furthermore, having your hearing and eyes protected will make your shooting easier and will help improve your enjoyment of the shooting sports.

8. Be Sure The Barrel Is Clear Of Obstructions Before Shooting

Before you load your firearm, open the action and be certain that no ammunition is in the chamber or magazine. Be sure the barrel is clear of any obstruction or something blocking the barrel. Even a small bit of mud, snow, excess oil or grease in the bore can cause dangerously increased pressures, causing the barrel to bulge or even burst on firing, which can cause injury to the shooter and those around you. Make it a habit to clean the bore and check for obstructions with a cleaning rod immediately before you shoot. If the noise or recoil on firing seems weak or doesn't seem quite "right," stop firing immediately and be sure to check that no obstruction or projectile has become lodged in the barrel.

Placing a smaller gauge or caliber cartridge into a gun (such as a 20-gauge shell in a 12-gauge shotgun) can result in the smaller cartridge falling into the barrel and acting as a bore obstruction when a cartridge of proper size is fired. This can cause a burst barrel or worse. This is really a case where "haste makes waste." You can easily avoid this type of accident by paying close attention to each cartridge you insert into your firearm.

9. Don't Alter Or Modify Your Gun, And Have Guns Serviced Regularly

Firearms are complicated devices that are designed by experts to work properly in their original condition. Any change made to a firearm after it is manufactured can make the gun dangerous and will usually void any factory warranties. Do not risk your safety or the safety of others by allowing an adult or yourself to change the trigger, safety, or other part of any firearm or allowing unqualified persons to repair or modify a gun. You'll usually ruin an expensive gun. Don't do it!

Your gun is a mechanical device that will not last forever and is subject to wear. Therefore, it requires frequent inspection, adjustment, and service. Check with the maker or manufacturer of your firearm for recommended servicing.

10. Learn The Mechanical And Handling Characteristics Of The Firearm You Are Using

Not all firearms are the same. The method of carrying and handling firearms changes based on the characteristics of each gun. Since guns can be so different, never handle any firearm without first having an adult instruct you in the particular type of firearm you are using, and the safe gun handling rules for loading, unloading, carrying and handling that firearm, and the rules of safe gun handling in general.

You and an adult should always read and refer to the instruction manual you received with your gun. If you have misplaced the manual, simply contact the manufacturer for a free copy.

Having a gun and handling it safely is a full-time job. You cannot guess; you cannot forget. You must know how to use, handle, and store your firearm safely. Do not use any firearm without adult supervision and having a complete understanding of its particular characteristics and safe use. There is no such thing as a foolproof gun.

Don't be afraid to speak up when it comes to gun safety. If you are not sure about something, ASK. If you observe anyone violating any safety rule, you should always speak up and ask them to follow these basic rules of gun safety!!

Safety Gear

Let's talk more about Rule #7 from the 10 Rules to Safe Gun Handling. The most important safety gear a shooter or hunter should have is a good pair of shooting glasses and high quality hearing protection.

Importance of Shooting Glasses

Whether you are shooting on the range or in the field, it is important to protect your eyes while you are shooting. To be sure you can clearly see your target, your eyes must stay focused and free of anything that might create problems with your eyesight. Shooting glasses are made to do just that.

Because your face is always very close to the gun you are shooting, you need to have something that protects your eyes from anything that may be blown back into your face while shooting. Glasses also keep dust or other objects out of your eyes if you are shooting in the field. Wind and sun can irritate your eyes. When your eyes get irritated, they sometimes water and cause your vision to be unclear. You must always have clear, focused vision when you are shooting to be sure you see your target and those around you.

Eye protection is required in organized shooting matches and some range masters allow any kind of eyewear to be worn. Other ranges and range masters may require glasses that have certain safety standards.

Features of Quality Shooting Glasses

- "Wrap around" design allows the lenses to cover both the front and sides of your face to keep most things from entering your eyes.
- Flexible, tough frames that won't break if the gun's recoil causes the gun to come back and hit the glasses.
- Lenses and frames that are made of a material that is tough, shatter-resistant or shatter-proof, such as polycarbonate.
- Frames that have some padding or material between the face and the frame to absorb sweat or to cushion the face if the gun's recoil causes the gun to come back and hit the glasses.
- Lenses that protect from ultraviolet rays if you are shooting outdoors.
- Some shooting glasses have interchangeable lenses that come in clear, yellow, or shaded lenses to help shoot in different lighting conditions.

No matter what shooting glasses you choose, just be sure you always wear them when you shoot. Without your eyes and good eyesight, you cannot see the target. Protect your eyes at all times.

Importance of Hearing Protection

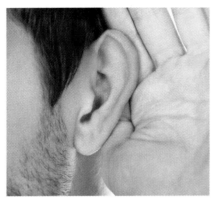

Your ears and your hearing are a very important sense you must protect. For this reason, when you shoot firearms that shoot cartridges or shells that use powder, you should always use hearing protection. Since air guns use only air to propel the projectile, the sound produced by the gun is not very loud. However, firearms such as smallbore and high-powered rifles and handguns, as well as shotguns, produce a lot of sound when they are fired.

How much sound does an average firearm make?

The average shotgun firing produces 130 dB of sound. That is almost as loud as a jet engine!!!! Sounds above 125 dB can cause pain in people, and hearing sounds over 85 dB over and over can cause hearing loss!

This means using hearing protection while you shoot is very important. Since several shooting sports require many shots over a given time, your ears are exposed to very loud sound over and over again. Without proper hearing protection, you can damage your ears and lose your hearing.

What types of hearing protection are there?

There are two basic forms of hearing protection devices, earplugs and earmuffs. Both will reduce the sound entering your ears and protect you from loud sounds such as gun blasts. However, there are different kinds of earplugs and earmuffs. Let's compare them.

Science of Sound

Sound is produced when something makes vibrations and the vibrations travel through the air or other medium. Those vibrations travel to your ear and the structures in your ear turn the vibrations into sound.

Sound is measured in decibels (dB). A decibel measures the intensity of the sound and involves using a scale based on the powers of 10. For example, total silence (no sound at all) is 0 dB. A sound 10 times louder than total silence is 10 dB. A sound 100 times louder is 20 dB, 1,000 times louder is 30 dB, and so on.

Common Sounds and Decibel Levels

Whisper	30 dB
Normal talking	60 dB
Hair dryer	70 dB
Average city traffic	80 dB
Chainsaw	110 dB
Rock concerts	110-140 dB
Close thunder	120 dB
Shotgun	130 dB
Jet engine	140 dB

Type of Device	Picture	Sound Reduction	Average cost
Disposable Foam Earplugs		25-31 dB	$ 0.50-1.00 a pair
Reuseable Earplugs		25-32 dB	$ 5.00-15.00 a pair
Custom molded Earplugs		26-30 dB	$ 15.00-150.00 a pair
Regular Shooting Muffs		21-30 dB	$15.00-30.00
Electronic Shooting Muffs		19-30 dB	$25.00-300.00

Hearing loss cannot be reversed. Protect your ears while you are young and you will hear well for a lifetime. You can choose whatever type of hearing protection you like. Just be sure you use it every time you shoot. You should also wear your hearing protection when you are not shooting when others around you are.

Range Safety

Many shooting sports, with the exception of hunting, occur on a shooting range of some kind. Therefore, it is important that you know and understand the rules, terms, and safety procedures for various shooting ranges. Although some ranges may use slightly different terms and rules, there are some common terms and rules you should know.

First and most important, all ranges expect shooters to follow the 10 Rules of Safe Gun Handling that were discussed at the beginning of this chapter. All shooters must make ALL of these rules a habit every time they shoot so they can be safe on any range or in any competition.

Range Terms

Range master or officer: Person in charge of the shooting range and who will supervise the shooting and give the shooters the commands.

Firing line: A line parallel to the targets, from behind which firearms are discharged.

Target line: A line parallel to the firing line along which targets are placed.

Misfire: Failure of a bullet cartridge to discharge after the firearm's firing pin has struck the primer.

Firing distance: The distance between the firing line and the target line.

Hot range: A range where shooters are able to actively shoot.

Cold range: A range where the shooting on the range has ceased and all firearms have been "made safe."

Range Commands to Know

"Stop"
Meaning: To tell all shooters to cease or stop firing immediately and unload their firearms.
Action: All shooters must immediately stop or cease firing and unload their firearms and make them safe.

"Start"
Meaning: To tell all shooters that shooting on the range may begin
Action: All shooters can pick up their firearms and proceed with the shooting competition or event.

"Shooters to the firing line"
Meaning: To tell shooters that they can load their firearms.
Action: Participants should load their firearms and wait for the next command.

"Is the line ready?"
Meaning: To ask if all shooters along the line are ready.
Action: All shooters not ready should tell the range officer. Sufficient time should then be allowed for the shooter(s) to complete their preparation.

"Ready on the right"
Meaning: To tell everyone that the shooters on the right side of the range have indicated they are ready.
Action: Any shooter not ready at this command may choose either to alert the range officer or complete the process of getting ready before the final command has been given.

"Ready on the left"
Meaning: To tell everyone the shooters on the left side of the range have indicated they are ready.
Action: Any shooter not ready at this command may choose either to alert the range officer or complete the process of getting ready before the final command has been given.

"Ready on the firing line"
Meaning: To tell all shooters that the range is about to be under live fire and that if anyone is not ready at this point, they should call the range officer.
Action: Await the next command.

"The range is now open, commence firing"
Meaning: To tell shooters the range is open for live fire and shooters can now shoot at the targets.
Action: The shooters can now shoot their given course of fire. Firing should continue for a given time period or until all participants have completed the given course of fire. Shooters finishing the course of fire should open their actions and bench their firearms, step behind the yellow "safe" line and wait quietly for remaining shooters to finish.

"Make & Show Safe"
Meaning: To tell shooters to unload or clear their firearms and place them on the bench.
Action: Clear or unload the firearm and have the firearm on the bench with the action open.

Safe Storage

It is very important that all firearms are stored safely and not be available to young shooters without adult supervision. Firearms should be locked in a safe, cabinet, or other type of storage device and should only be able to be opened by an adult. There are other safety devices to make sure firearms are unable to be fired or show the firearm is unloaded.

Barrel indicators are used in many air rifles or smallbore rifles to show the guns are unloaded. These indicators are commonly made of very heavy monofilament such as the string used in "weed whackers." Bright color indicators, like orange or red, are best because they can easily be spotted quickly. When the air gun or smallbore firearm is unloaded, the indicator should be placed into the barrel so one end comes out of the breech and the other out of the muzzle.

The National Shooting Sports Foundation (NSSF) has organized Project Child Safe. This project stresses the importance of storing firearms safely and away from children. It also is meant to educate families and communities about safe gun handling and storage. Find out more at www.projectchildsafe.org.

Gun locks, like the locks provided by Project Child Safe and most gun manufacturers, are an effective way to store firearms safely, so they cannot be fired. All stored firearms should have a gun lock that is locked through the action or in a way that keeps the gun from being loaded and fired. Here are some examples of how gun locks can be used on different types of firearms.

Location of gun lock on a semi-auto or bolt action rifle.

Location of gun lock on a semi-auto or pump action shotgun.

Location of gun lock on a semi-auto pistol.

Firearms safety is THE most important factor in the shooting sports. Firearms safety is up to you!! You must be aware of ALL of the safety rules and make them a habit every time you shoot. Remember, you must ALWAYS shoot with adult supervision. Shooting firearms can be a fun and an enjoyable activity. Guns are not toys and can be very dangerous if not handled safely!

When you shoot, be with a responsible adult, follow the rules of firearms safety, and wear the proper safety gear, you can enjoy any shooting sport you wish to participate in. As this book has mentioned over and over, shooting sports are some of the safest activities you can participate in, but it is up to you to keep them safe by doing your part in following these safety rules.

CHAPTER 5

FIRST IN AIR

YOUR SHOOTING SPORTS

LOCAL SHOOTING ORGANIZATIONS

STATE AND NATIONAL COMPETITIONS

WWW.USASHOOTING.ORG   WWW.USASHOOTING.ORG

USA SHOOTING NATIONAL CHAMPION
SHOTGUN
COLORADO SPRINGS, COLORADO

Photo credit: USA Shooting Sports

JUNIOR OLYMPICS

Photo credit: USA Shooting Sports

COLLEGE TEAM

Photo credit: USA Shooting Sports

SHOOTING JOURNEY

INTERNATIONAL AND OLYMPIC SHOOTING

Photo credit: USA Shooting Sports

PROFESSIONAL SHOOTING

Photo credit: USA Shooting Sports

HUNTING

Where Can Shooting Sports Lead?

At this point, you should have a good understanding of different shooting sports that are available to you. You can choose to participate in shooting sports just for fun and to spend time with family and friends enjoying something that you all can do together. If you decide you really like the shooting sports and want to compete, there are many options that can lead to great rewards.

This final chapter explains what you can do as you progress in the shooting sports. If you commit to practice and get serious about shooting sports, there is no telling how far these sports can take you. It is up to you how you want to compete. If you do decide to set high goals for yourself and strive to be successful, you might become a USA Olympic shooter.

Planning Your Journey

You and your parent or other responsible adult should begin to explore what shooting sports you are interested in and would like to pursue. Whether it is air gun, smallbore, or shotgun sports, you can take many routes as you begin your path down the shooting sports road. Let's look at the steps you can take as you make your shooting sports journey.

STEP #1 Find Local Organizations and Shooting Clubs

If you are at the very beginning of your journey, find a local organization or shooting club that will help you get started. There are many local organizations and clubs that beginning shooters can join to learn more about shooting sports. 4-H National Shooting Sports clubs are a place to begin because 4-H is dedicated to teaching and developing young people's interest in shooting. Most 4-H shooting clubs offer a variety of shooting sports, from air guns, shotguns, smallbore, and even archery. Organizations like the Civilian Marksmanship Program (CMP) specialize in sports like air gun and smallbore. Scholastic Clay Target Program (SCTP), American Trapshooting Association, and the National Skeet Shooting Association clubs participate in the shotgun sports.

There are many national, non-profit conservation organizations that sponsor and organize youth shooting clubs and events. These organizations have chapters or clubs in most states. These organizations can be a place to start. Here is some brief information about a few of these non-profit organizations.

Pheasants Forever (PF) and Quail Forever (QF)

PF and QF is an organization that is dedicated to the conservation of pheasant, quail and other wildlife habitat. They are also dedicated to encouraging young people to participate in shooting and conservation. Their shooting program is called Forever Shooting Sports. The Forever Shooting Sports program is a gateway for youngsters into the world of shooting and upland hunting...and an introduction to the importance of upland conservation. PF and QF have chapters in most states that can help you on a local level. You can find out more about Forever Shooting Sports at http://www.pheasantsforever.org/Youth/Forever-Shooting-Sports.aspx

Safari Club International Foundation (SCIF)

The Safari Club International Foundation is a national organization dedicated to educating youth and protecting our hunting heritage. SCI Foundation operates the American Wilderness Leadership School (AWLS) in Jackson, Wyoming. The American Wilderness Leadership School has a seven-day student program for youth ages 16-18. The student program presents a base knowledge of wildlife ecology and conservation. Students participate in shooting sports such as shotgun, rifle, pistol, and archery.

SCIF also partners with The Salvation Army Outdoors (TSAO) to bring conservation education into The Salvation Army youth character development programs for youth. Recreation activities being developed in TSAO camps and programs include shooting sports. TSAO staff are trained at the SCI Foundation American Wilderness Leadership School and AWLS staff has provided training to TSAO staff at Salvation Army facilities in the Midwest. To find out more about SCIF's youth programs go to http://www.safariclubfoundation.org/education/youthprograms.

Civilian Marksmanship Program (CMP)

CMP is a non-profit organization that is dedicated to promoting firearms safety and marksmanship training, especially for youth. CMP is not only involved in air guns, they also organize smallbore events. The CMP has a website that can help you find a club that may help you get started in the smallbore shooting sports.

The CMP holds air gun and rimfire events at both of their locations in Port Clinton, Ohio, and Anniston, Alabama. Visit the CMP website, http://www.thecmp.org/, to find out more about CMP. You can also use their club finder to locate a shooting club near you. Click the "Clubs" link on the homepage to find the Find a CMP Affiliated Club link.

4-H Shooting Sports

Most people are familiar with 4-H and the clubs associated with 4-H. However, you may not realize that 4-H has a wonderful shooting sports program. You can join a 4-H shooting sports club and participate in the

various air gun, rimfire, and shotgun events that may be held at the state and local levels where you live.

To find a 4-H shooting sports club near you, go to the national 4-H shooting sports website at www.4-hshootingsports.org/ and click on the "Find 4-H Shooting Sports in your Area" button at the top of the page. This will take you to a page with the coordinators for each state. You can then contact your state coordinator and find a club near you.

USA Shooting

 USA Shooting sponsors the National Junior Olympic program which provides competitions year-round for shooters. The program runs matches throughout the country, making it accessible for all interested juniors. These programs include air rifle and air pistol. There are state and national competitions for 3-position air rifle and air pistol, which includes the Progressive-Position Pistol program. The Junior Olympic Shooting programs also include smallbore and shotgun. You can find out more about the Junior Olympic program at http://www.usashooting.org/7-events/njosc.

Junior shooters are able to participate in State Competitions sanctioned by USA Shooting, allowing them the chance to receive an invitation to then shoot at the National Junior Olympic Championships hosted by USA Shooting in Colorado Springs, Colorado. The National Junior Olympic Shotgun program runs from late spring to mid-summer, with the NJOSC held in June. To find out more about the National Junior Olympic Program, go to http://www.usashooting.org/7-events/njosc. USA Shooting also has a tool to find shooting clubs to help you get involved. This tool can be found at http://www.usashooting.org/7-events/locateaclub.

Scholastic Shooting Sports Foundation (SSSF)

 The Scholastic Shooting Sports Foundation (SSSF) offers a great shooting program for youth. The SSSF offers the Scholastic Pistol Program (SPP) which involves speed shooting on steel targets. The program is for kids from 12 years old through college and offers the opportunity to safely participate in an exciting team-based sport. The program uses both smallbore or rimfire pistols, as well as centerfire pistols. Shooters shoot rectangular and circular steel plates in timed events. To find out more about SPP, go to http://sssfonline.org/scholastic-pistol-program-spp/.

The Scholastic Shooting Sports Foundation (SSSF) also sponsors the largest and most exciting clay target program for youth in the United States. The organization oversees the Scholastic Clay Target Program (SCTP). The SCTP provides kids from elementary grades through high school and college with the opportunity to participate in the fun and challenging sports of Trap, Skeet, and Sporting Clays, as well as the Olympic disciplines of Bunker Trap, Trap Doubles, and International Skeet. SSSF is the official feeder program to USA Shooting and a path to the U.S. Olympic Shooting Team. Find out more about SCTP at http://sssfonline.org/scholastic-clay-target-program/.

Boy Scouts

The Boy Scouts of America (BSA) provide programs to youth age 7 to 21 that are designed to build Citizenship, Character, Leadership, and Fitness. Scouting uses experiential learning experiences, such as Shooting Sports, to build and reinforce these four core aims of Scouting.

The Shooting Sports program conducted by the BSA is a progressive skill development program with the primary goal of teaching youth to be safe and responsible when handling firearms. Below are the shooting sports activities provided in each of the BSA programs:

Cub Scouts (for boys 8 to 10 years of age)
* BB gun program
* .177 caliber air rifle shooting program
* Archery program

Boy Scouts (for boys 11 to 18 years of age)
* .22 caliber, bolt action rifle program and merit badge opportunity
* 20-, 16-, or 12-guage semi-automatic shotgun program including five stand, trap, and sporting clays and merit badge opportunity
* Muzzleloading rifle
* 10- gauge muzzleloading shotgun
* .22 caliber pistols at approved camps only
* Archery program

Venturers and Sea Scouts (co-ed programs for youth 14 to 21 years of age)
* Any cartridge-firing rifle with open, scope, or dot sights
* 20-, 16-, or 12-guage semi-automatic shotgun program including five stand, trap, and sporting clays and merit badge program
* Muzzleloading rifle
* 10- gauge muzzleloading shotgun
* Muzzleloading pistol
* Any pistol that meets the requirements of the competitive rule book for the course of competition
* Archery program

American Legion Junior Shooting Sports Program

The American Legion Junior Shooting Sports Program is a gun safety education and marksmanship program that encompasses the basic elements of safety, education, enjoyment, and competition. Both males and females can participate, through Legion sponsorship; disabled youth are encouraged to join, as competitive shooting is a sport that creates an equal playing field for all competitors. Contact your local Legion post, Sons of The American Legion squadron or Auxiliary unit for information about affiliating as a club or individual. You can also visit http://www.legion.org/shooting/about.

National Wild Turkey Federation (NWTF)

The NWTF is an organization dedicated to the conservation of the wild turkey and the preservation of our hunting heritage. The NWTF has the JAKES Take Aim program. The goal of the JAKES Take Aim program is to present opportunities for youth age 17 and younger to try target shooting, clay target shooting, and shotgunning in a safe, fun environment. To find out more about the NWTF's JAKES Take Aim program, go to http://www.nwtf.org/jakes/take_aim/.

Whitetails Unlimited (WU)

WU is an organization with a mission to conserve and make the habitat of the white-tailed deer better. The organization has developed Kids on Target programs to encourage youth to get involved in the shooting sports. You can find out more about Whitetails Unlimited's Kids on Target at http://www.whitetailsunlimited.com/resources/kids_on_target/.

Ducks Unlimited (DU)

DU is a conservation organization committed to conserving important habitat for waterfowl. The organization is dedicated to introducing the next generation to shooting and hunting. DU has the Greenwing program that is focused on youth. DU chapters nationwide organize Greenwing youth events. To find out more go to http://www.ducks.org/how-to-help/membership/greenwings/greenwing-events?poe=greenwingRHS.

Mule Deer Foundation (MDF)

The mission of the Mule Deer Foundation is to ensure the conservation of mule deer, black-tailed deer and their habitat. The MDF is also dedicated to getting youth involved in shooting and hunting. MDF's M.U.L.E.Y. (Mindful, Understanding, Legal and Ethical Youth) program organizes youth events that allow youth to participate in the shooting sports. To find out more about MDF's M.U.L.E.Y. program, go to http://www.muledeer.org/MULEY.

Rocky Mountain Elk Foundation (RMEF)

RMEF is a conservation organization that has a mission to ensure the future of elk, other wildlife, their habitat, and our hunting heritage. The Rocky Mountain Elk Foundation has several outreach programs to help people learn more about our hunting heritage and the role hunters play in conserving wildlife and their habitat. One outreach program is SAFE (Shooting Access For Everyone). SAFE events introduce young and novice shooters to safe and responsible firearm use, educate newcomers about the hunter's role in conservation and the North American Wildlife Conservation Model. To find out more go to http://www.rmef.org/Conservation/HuntingHeritagePrograms.aspx.

Quality Deer Management Association (QDMA)

The mission of the QDMA is similar to that of the RMEF but with the focus on deer. The QDMA is committed to ensuring the future of white-tailed deer, wildlife habitat, and our hunting heritage. QDMA's youth initiative is the Rack Pack. This Rack Pack strives to create a program that is fun and exciting through creative methods including field days, social media, games, contests, hunts, shooting experiences, firearms safety instruction and competitions. Find out more at http://rackpack.qdma.com/introduction.

Wild Sheep Foundation

The Wild Sheep Foundation is dedicated to improving wild sheep populations, promoting wildlife management, and educating the public and youth on the conservation benefits of hunting. The Wild Sheep Foundation holds Youth Wildlife Conservation Experiences (YWCE) that offer youth a glimpse into different aspects of conservation, the shooting sports, and the outdoors. Find out more at http://www.wildsheepfoundation.org/Page.php/cp/YWCE.

Youth Shooting Sports Alliance (YSSA)

The YSSA is an organization that promotes youth and the shooting sports by identifying and supporting the needs of successful and safe shooters. They provide leadership in the development and promotion of family-friendly shooting range facilities to encourage continued participation in the shooting sports. Their website has a tool to find shooting opportunities near your home. Go to http://youthshootingsa.com/home.

USA Youth Education in Shooting Sports (USAYESS)

USA Youth Education in Shooting Sports is dedicated to growing competitive youth shooting teams primarily through partnerships with Key Conservation Groups as well as local, state, regional, and national competitive youth shooting organizations. USAYESS provides events which showcase safety of equipment and outdoor activities in a fun-filled atmosphere. Find out more about USAYESS at http://usayess.org/.

Youth Target Foundation (YTF)

The Youth Target Foundation is an organization created to involve youth in shooting sports. YTF has created high school and middle school competitive clay target teams, designed training programs for youth, parents, coaches, and volunteers, and set up professional training clinics. YTF is dedicated to educating youth and to helping parents become more involved in a sport that we know the youth will love. Check out more at http://www.youthtargetfoundation.com/.

U.S. Sportsmens Alliance (USSA)

The USSA is an organization that is passionate about protecting our hunting rights and heritage. The USSA organizes and sponsors the Trailblazer Adventure Program. The Trailblazer Adventure Program is the largest outdoor program of its kind and has introduced more than 1.7 million youth to the thrill of outdoor sports since 2001! Through this exciting program, seasoned sportsmen and wildlife professionals provide hands-on firearms safety lessons, fishing instruction, archery programs, trapping demonstrations, and more. Find out more at http://www.ussportsmen.org/youth-programs/.

National Rifle Association (NRA)

The NRA sponsors and organizes competitive shooting programs across the country. The programs include both precision and sporter air rifle competitions. The NRA also has a great way for shooters to begin at home. The NRA's Home Air Gun Program Introduction brings marksmanship activities directly to the community. This guide is to provide parents, teachers, activity and club leaders with information and guidance on BB and air gun shooting sports. It also guides you on how to select a BB or air gun and how to construct permanent ranges and what portable ranges are available. In addition it explains what support equipment that is needed and a vendor resource list. You can print out their Home Air Gun Program by visiting http://youth.nra.org/documents/pdf/youth/NRA_HomeAG_web02.pdf.

Because of this mission, the NRA has a Competitive Shooting Division that offers a wide range of shooting activities for everyone from beginners to professional shooters. These activities also include smallbore and shotgun competitions. To find out more about how to get involved in NRA's competitions check out the NRA's website at http://compete.nra.org/.

National Shooting Sports Foundation (NSSF)

The National Shooting Sports Foundation (NSSF) is the trade association for the firearms industry. Its mission is to promote, protect, and preserve hunting and the shooting sports. The NSSF has programs to help new shooters to begin their journey into the shooting sports.

The NSSF's First Shots program has helped ranges across the country introduce thousands of individuals to shooting and firearms safety. The program is hosted by independent shooting facilities and provides participants with a comprehensive introduction to shooting by qualified range operators and instructors that includes firearms safety, local ownership requirements, shooting fundamentals, hands-on instruction, and how and where to continue.

The NSSF Rimfire Challenge is a .22 rifle and pistol program created to introduce new people to the shooting sports and provide a pathway to shooting competition. The NSSF Rimfire Challenge can provide individuals or families with a fun and exciting first-time shooting experience. Shooting ranges can use the concept as a Second Round component to NSSF's First Shots program.

Amateur Trapshooting Association (ATA)

Amateur Trapshooting Association (ATA) is the official organization of the sport of Trapshooting. Founded in 1889, the ATA acts as the "protector" of the sport of trapshooting and oversees the rules and regulations of American trapshooting. The ATA is also dedicated to increasing participation in the sport and has developed a youth program to help encourage young people to get involved in trapshooting.

The official youth program of the ATA is AIM. AIM stands for Academics, Integrity, and Marksmanship. Participants of AIM will enjoy the thrill of shooting registered competition on a level playing field as an individual and/or as a team. The purpose of AIM is to provide a safe and positive experience with firearms and registered trapshooting for youth, from elementary age through college age. AIM encourages good sportsmanship and personal responsibility through competition while establishing the foundation to make trapshooting a lifelong pasttime. To find out more about the AIM program visit http://www.aim4ata.com/content/about.html. The ATA also has a website to help beginning shooters find a local gun club or trap range where they can go to get started. That website is http://www.shootata.com/Shoots,Clubs,StatesZones.aspx.

National Skeet Shooting Association (NSSA)

Founded in 1928 and headquartered in San Antonio, Texas, the National Skeet Shooting Association is the largest organization in the world dedicated solely to the sport of skeet shooting. The NSSA is dedicated to the development of the sport at all levels of participation. Shooters who want to compete can enter fun shoots and skeet shooting tournaments. NSSA Youth Camps are planned around the country to introduce young shooters to the game of skeet, teach fundamental shooting skills, and reinforce safe gun handling practices. Check out their website at http://www.nssa-nsca.org/index.php/nssa-skeet-shooting/.

National Sporting Clays Association (NSCA)

NSCA is the largest Sporting Clays association in the world and oversees the sport in the U.S. The organization keeps records of scores in competition, registers shoots for clubs and associations, holds the National Championship each year, and provides many awards for outstanding achievements. New shooters can check out their website for information at http://www.nssa-nsca.org/index.php/nsca-sporting-clays-shooting/new-to-sporting-clays/.

USA High School Clay Target League

The USA High School Clay Target League is a 501(c)(3) non-profit corporation and the independent provider of shooting sports as an extracurricular co-ed activity to high schools for students in grades six through twelve who have their firearms safety certification. To find out more about the USA High School Clay Target League and how to get involved, visit http://www.usaclaytarget.com/.

If you are new to the shooting sports, check out any of these fine organizations and they can help you start your journey. The key is to find an organization that participates in the shooting sport you are interested in. Once you find an organization, don't be shy about asking for help as you get started. These organizations are dedicated and committed to assisting young shooters.

If you have been shooting for a while and you are pretty good, maybe you now want to compete against other shooters. This is the next step on your shooting sports journey. There are many opportunities for shooters of any skill range to compete in the shooting sports. Many of the organizations highlighted in this book organize regional, state, and national competitions.

Photo credit: USA Shooting Sports

Competitions can be individual or a team event. If you do not have a team, you can still participate and compete as an individual. If you are part of a shooting club, members in your club can compete as a team. There are many different competitions available to shooters. The key is to find a competition near your home and try it. Some people love to shoot competitively, while others just like shooting for fun. You will never know until you give it a try.

It is impossible to highlight all state and national shooting events because there are so many. Different organizations sponsor different state and national competitions. This chapter will only highlight a few of the most common opportunities for shooters at the national level. Check with your local clubs to find information about competitions in your state.

Daisy National BB Gun Championship Match

Daisy National BB Gun Championship Match, or Daisy Nationals, is the national match for Daisy sponsored 5-meter BB gun marksmanship programs held around the country. Only those teams that come in first, second, or third place at a sanctioned state match qualify to attend and compete in the Daisy Nationals.

Photo credit: Daisy

You can be part of a 5-meter BB gun team by joining an organization that shoots 5-meter BB gun competitions such as 4-H, the American Legion, Royal Rangers, Boy Scouts, as well as other groups that train and sponsor shooting teams.

At the nationals, about 450 young people ages 8 to 15 compete using the single-shot BB gun called the Daisy AVANTI Champion, Model 499. They shoot in four positions and take a safety exam. The highest scoring teams and individuals are recognized with awards. You can find out more about the Daisy BB Gun Nationals at www.daisy.com/daisynationals.

4-H Shooting Sports National Championship

This national 4-H shooting competition is an invitational, which means you must qualify and be invited to compete. Most national competitions are organized this way. To qualify for the 4-H National Championship, you must shoot a qualifying score at a qualifying shooting event in your state.

The 4-H shooting Sports National Championship has several shooting sports events. These events include air pistol, air rifle, .22 rifle, .22 pistol, shotgun, muzzleloader, archery, and hunting skills. This event is typically held in Grand Island, Nebraska. To find out more about this event visit http://4h.unl.edu/ntlshootingsportsinvitational.

CMP State and National Matches

The Civilian Marksmanship Program (CMP) sponsor state, regional, and national matches for 3 position air rifle (3PAR). Individuals and teams can compete in the state or region matches to qualify for the national championships. CMP sponsors the national rimfire sporter championship. This national match is different because anyone can compete in three different rifle classes. The National Rimfire Sporter Match at Camp Perry offers a great opportunity to fire a fun-oriented match with your favorite rimfire rifle. Find out more at http://thecmp.org/competitions/club-sanctioned-events/rimfire-sporter/.

Scholastic Shooting Sports Foundation's (SSSF) National Matches

The SSSF sponsors state, regional, and national matches for the Scholastic Clay Target Program (SCTP) and the Scholastic Pistol Program (SPP). These events are for teams to compete at the state or regional level so they can qualify to attend the national matches for each of these programs. The SCTP matches feature Trap, Skeet, and Sporting Clays, as well as the Olympic disciplines of Bunker Trap, Trap Doubles, and International Skeet. The SPP matches feature competition in a centerfire and/or a rimfire division with targets that are steel circle or rectangular plates. Find out more about the SSSF at http://sssfonline.org/.

USA Shooting National Matches

USA Shooting sponsors and organizes national shoots as part of their shooting programs. Like other national competitions, shooters must qualify at a state or regional competition. National events are held in air rifle, air pistol, smallbore, and shotgun. Shooting in the USA Shooting's national competitions is a way for aspiring shooters to take another big step in their shooting sports journey.

STEP #3 Compete in the National Junior Olympic Program

The National Junior Olympic program provides competitions year-round for shooters. The program runs matches throughout the country, making it accessible for all interested juniors. Junior shooters are able to participate in state competitions sanctioned by USA Shooting, allowing them the chance to receive an invitation to shoot at the National Junior Olympic Championships hosted by USA Shooting in Colorado Springs, Colorado. The program is an important step in the shooting sports journey of an athlete who is serious about competing in the shooting sports. Junior

Olympic goals are to allow the skilled junior athletes to obtain national competitive experience and to appoint the top finishers to the National Junior Team.

The National Junior Olympic program includes air rifle, air pistol, smallbore rifle, smallbore pistol, and shotgun events. The National Junior Olympic Rifle & Pistol program runs from fall to early spring, with the National Junior Olympic Shooting Championships (NJOSC) held in April. The National Junior Olympic Shotgun program runs from late spring to mid-summer, with the National Junior Olympic Shooting Championships (NJOSC) held in June. You can find out more at http://www. usashooting.org/7-events/njosc.

STEP #4 Shoot on a Team at the College Level

A lot of people do not realize that many colleges have shooting sports teams as part of their athletic programs. Almost 300 colleges and universities in the U.S. have shooting programs. Since the shooting sports are a sport just like any other sport such as basketball, football, volleyball, or soccer, many colleges and universities have shooting teams as well. You can get college scholarships to participate in some of the shooting sports, just like other sports.

College programs include all of the various events in the shooting sports such as rifle, pistol, and shotgun. There is an NCAA Rifle Championship, just like other NCAA championship events! In addition to the NCAA, there are two organizations that sponsor and promote intercollegiate shooting events.

NRA The NRA sponsors many intercollegiate shooting events and matches. The events include both rifle and pistol events in air and smallbore categories. These matches include both individual and team competitions. The NRA has an online publication that is a resource for learning more about collegiate shooting programs. You can access it at http:// issuu.com/compshoot/docs/nracollegiate/1.

 The other organization that sponsors collegiate shooting is the Association of College Unions International (ACUI). The ACUI Recreation Program annually sponsors the ACUI Collegiate Clay Target Championships, which is open to full-time college students. The championships are the only national collegiate event featuring all six events: International Skeet and Trap, American Skeet and Trap, Five-Stand, and Sporting Clays. The NRA sponsors and funds the international events in trap and skeet and oversees the welfare of collegiate shotgun shooting programs. Find out more about this program at http://www.acui.org/claytargets/.

STEP #5 Be a Part of Team USA's Shooting Team

Shooting is an international sport. Shooting sports are very popular in many countries and international competitions are held for countries to compete against one another. USA Shooting selects shooters from the winners of the national competitions to be part of Team USA's shooting teams for the different events.

Every four years, people anticipate the worldwide competition of the Olympic Games. Olympic athletes are some of the most elite athletes in the world. Some people do not realize that the shooting sports are popular events at each Olympic Games. The shooting sports were part of the modern Olympic Games from the beginning.

French nobleman Baron Pierre de Coubertin organized the first modern Olympic Games in 1896 in Athens, Greece. It began with nine competitive sports, including shooting. A former French pistol champion, de Coubertin supported including four pistol and two high-power rifle events on the Olympic program.

Shooting events have been a part of all the Olympic Games except the 1904 Games in St. Louis, Missouri, and the 1928 Olympic Games in Amsterdam. The number of Olympic shooting events has ranged from a low of two at the 1932 Los Angeles Games to a high of 21 events in Atwerp in 1920. Beginning in 2008 at the Beijing Olympic Games, the Olympic program now includes 15 events: six for women and nine for men. The athletes are divided into shotgun, rifle, and pistol disciplines.

USA Shooting was chartered in April 1995 by the United States Olympic Committee as the National Governing Body for the sport of shooting. The organization implements and manages development programs and sanctions events at the local, state, regional, and national levels. Headquartered in Colorado Springs, Colorado, at the U.S. Olympic Training Center, USA Shooting has a full-time staff dedicated to furthering the sport and supporting athletes and members of the organization.

Path to the Olympics

If your goal is to be on Team USA's Shooting Team, the best way to achieve that goal is to participate in the National Junior Olympic Shooting Program. If you compete and qualify for the National Junior Olympic Shooting Championships, you can shoot your way onto the National Junior Olympic team. By competing on the National Junior Olympic team, you have the

opportunity to compete in higher level competitions, sharpen your shooting skills even further, and eventually shoot good enough to make the National Olympic Shooting team and compete in the Olympic Games!!

What Events to Practice to Reach the Olympics

Pistol
- Men's 10m Air Pistol
- Women's 10m Air Pistol
- Men's 25m Rapid Fire Pistol
- Women's 25m Sport Pistol
- Men's 50m Free Pistol

Rifle
- Men's 10m Air Rifle
- Women's 10m Air Rifle
- Men's 50m Rifle Three Position
- Women's 50m Rifle Three Position
- Men's 50m Rifle Prone

Shotgun
- Men's Skeet
- Women's Skeet
- Men's Trap
- Women's Trap
- Men's Double Trap

Only a few can make the National Olympic Shooting team, but you can do it with a lot of practice and dedication. Unlike many of the other Olympic sports, shooting does not require the athlete to be big, strong, or fast. You just need to be a skilled shooter! Anyone can achieve that if they work at it. So…why not you? You could be the next Olympic gold medalist at an upcoming Olympic Games.

Other Places the Shooting Sports Journey Can Lead

Even if you do not make it to the Olympic team, shooting can still lead to many opportunities in your life. Shooting is a lifetime sport, which means you can enjoy shooting the rest of your life, no matter your age. Here are opportunities where shooting can lead you.

Professional Shooting

There is a growing number of people who actually make money using their shooting skills. Professional shooters are shooters who have become very good at shooting competitions and win large professional shooting competitions that pay out money to the winners. There are many different types of professional events ranging from handguns to shotguns.

Some of these shooters sign contracts and get paid by companies, such as gun manufacturers, to represent their companies when they shoot in these professional competitions. Sometimes companies sponsor shooters by providing money if they wear the company's logo or patch on their clothing. Just like you see stickers and logos on the race cars in a NASCAR race, you can see professional shooters with several patches, logos, and company names on their shirts and hats.

Professional shooter Dave Miller

Professional shooting is not for everyone, but it is something you may consider if you want to continue to shoot competitively and make money doing it!!

Lifetime of Hunting

As was stated earlier in the book, hunting is a shooting sport. Your shooting sports journey can continue the rest of your life by enjoying the sport of hunting. Skilled shooters are often the best and most successful hunters because they have learned the necessary skills to cleanly harvest game animals. Ethical hunters strive to make quick, clean harvests of the game animals they hunt. You must continue to practice and keep your shooting skills sharp to make those clean harvests.

Hunting is an extremely important tool to manage wildlife populations. Hunting is important for all wildlife, not just game animals. If the balance of predators and herbivores becomes unbalanced, the whole ecosystem and all of the wildlife in that ecosystem are in danger. Hunting laws and regulations are set by professionals and scientists who monitor wildlife populations. Harvest limits and game bag regulations are closely set based on this population information.

There is nothing more rewarding than knowing you have the shooting skills necessary to be a skilled, responsible hunter and doing your part to help keep wildlife populations healthy. You can continue having these rewarding experiences for the rest of your life.

End of the Book but Not Your Journey

It is hoped that this book provided information that sparks your interest in shooting sports or maybe just helps to further your shooting sports journey. Shooting sports are wonderful and rewarding activities that anyone can enjoy. No matter if you start with a BB gun plinking cans with your family, you can take the shooting sports journey as far as you would like.

OutdoorIQ, Pheasants Forever, the Safari Club International Foundation, and Hunter Legacy Fund hope that by making this book possible, you are encouraged to either begin a journey into the shooting sports or further your journey. Regardless of how far you take your journey, shooting is a sport you can enjoy for a lifetime. Shooting is enjoyed by all ages and generations. Shoot responsibly and safely with family and friends and build relationships that will last a lifetime.

How to Get Involved in Air Gun Sports

If you are interested in exploring or participating in an air gun shooting sport, you just need to find an organization that will help you get started. There are many organizations that have wonderful shooting sports programs and welcome new shooters.

Below are a few of the main organizations that young shooters can contact to begin their air gun shooting experience. To find out more details about each of the organizations below, check out the page number from Chapter 5 under the organization's name.

Civilian Marksmanship Program (CMP)
Page 105

American Legion Jr.
Shooting Sports Program
Page 107

4-H Shooting Sports
Page 105

Boy Scouts
Page 107

USA Shooting
Page 106

National Rifle Association (NRA)
Page 110

How to Get Involved in Smallbore Sports

Below are a few of the main organizations that young shooters can contact to begin their smallbore shooting experience. To find out more details about each of the organizations below, check out the page number from Chapter 5 next to the organization's name and/or logo.

Civilian Marksmanship Program (CMP)
Page 105

Boy Scouts
Page 107

4-H Shooting Sports
Page 105

National Rifle Association (NRA)
Page 110

USA Shooting
Page 106

Scholastic Shooting Sports
Foundation (SSSF)
Page 106

National Shooting Sports Foundation
Page 110

How to Get Involved in Shotgun Sports

If you would like to get involved in a shotgun shooting sport, there are organizations that can help you get started. These organizations have programs that promote these shotgun sports and are dedicated to help new shooters enter these wonderful sports. Here are a few of the main organizations that beginning shooters can contact to get involved in the shotgun shooting sports.

Scholastic Shooting Sports Foundation (SSSF)
Page 106

Amateur Trapshooting Association (ATA)
Page 110

4-H Shooting Sports
Page 105

National Skeet Shooting Association (NSSA)
Page 111

USA Shooting
Page 106

National Sporting Clays Association (NSCA)
Page 111

Educational Online Videos and Web Resources For the Shooting Sports

This book has hopefully given you some great information to increase your knowledge of the shooting sports. However, it is impossible to cover every aspect of the shooting sports. Therefore, we want to include some online video and web resources you can check out to learn even more!

Here are several web resources and online videos that will provide you with even more information to help you on your shooting sports journey. Check them out!!!

USA Shooting

- Olympic Shooting Information and Videos of events - http://www.usashooting.org/about/olympic-games

- Olympic Shooting Sports video - http://www.brainshark.com/usashooting/vu?pi=zFVz12Negz521yz0&intk=138208560

- Olympic Shooting Highlight video - https://www.youtube.com/watch?v=DWXZ6DQKjU&feature=youtube

- USA Shooting's YouTube Channel - https://www.youtube.com/user/USAShootingTeam

- Safety Video - http://www.usashooting.org/11-resources/safetytipsandvideo

- Online Training for USAS safety training course - http://www.brainshark.com/usashooting/UnlockedSafeSportPolicy

National Shooting Sports Foundation (NSSF)

- NSSF's YouTube Channel - https://www.youtube.com/user/TheNSSF/videos

- First Shots Program info - http://www.nssf.org/FirstShots/NewShooters/

Websites to Find Clubs and Shooting Ranges

- NSSF's Find a Range - Find a Range webpage - http://wheretoshoot.org/Find_Range/index.asp

- CMP's Club Search - https://ct.thecmp.org/app/v1/index.php?do=clubSearch

- USA Shooting Find a Club - http://www.usashooting.org/7-events/locateaclub

- YSSA's Youth Shooting Sports Program Directory - http://www.youthshootingsa.com/

- 4-H Shooting Sports State Contacts - http://www.4-hshootingsports.org/state_contacts.php

Ultimate Youth Shooting Sports Guide Reviewer Acknowledgements

OutdoorIQ thanks and acknowledges those who reviewed the content of this book. We asked the experts and leaders in various shooting sports organizations and industry to review the content of this book for accuracy and detail. A big thank you goes out to the following reviewers.

Mike Theimer – USA Shooting – Youth Programs & Athlete Development Manager

Chip Hunnicut – Crosman – Marketing Manager

Joe Murfin – Daisy Outdoor Products – V.P. Public Relations

Steve Cooper – Civilian Marksmanship Program (CMP) – Marketing Manager

Bill Brassard Jr. – National Shooting Sports Foundation – Director of Communications

Ben Berka – Scholastic Shooting Sports Foundation (SSSF) – President & Executive Director

Tom Wondrash – Scholastic Clay Target Program (SCTP) – SCTP National Program Director

Scott Moore – Scholastic Pistol Program (SPP) – SPP National Program Director

Tammy Mowry – Scholastic Pistol Program – SPP Program Manager

Sue Hankner – Safari Club International Foundation – Director of Education

Todd Roggenkamp – Safari Club International Foundation – Deputy Director of Education

John Linquist – Pheasants Forever/Qual Forever – Forever Shooting Sports National Coordinator

Cheryl Riley – Pheasants Forever/Quail Forever – V.P. of Education

Shawna Pantzke – Pheasants Forever and Quail Forever National Youth Leadership Council – President

Doug Sandstrom – Training Officer – Minnesota Department of Natural Resources

Pat Wellen – Boy Scouts of America – Director of Research & Program Innovation

Conrad Arnold – National 4-H Shooting Sports – Program Coordinator

Shooting Sports Guide Index